THEOLOGY *for* EVERYMAN

THEOLOGY

for

EVERYMAN

By

Dr. John H. Gerstner

Soli Deo Gloria Publications
...for instruction in righteousness...

Soli Deo Gloria Publications
213 W. Vincent Street, Ligonier, PA 15658
(412) 238-7741

*

Theology for Everyman was first published
by Moody Press in 1965.

This Soli Deo Gloria reprint is 1991.

*

ISBN 1-877611-40-9

To
Rachel Gwen,
a very young theologian

Table of Contents

CHAPTER I

Everyman Must Be a Theologian

LAYMEN SOMETIMES THINK they need not be theologians. That, however, is a very great mistake. They do need to be theologians; at least, they should be amateur theologians. In fact, that is the one vocation every man is obliged to follow. A layman does not need to be a plumber, a carpenter, a lawyer, a doctor, a teacher, a laborer, a housewife. These are all possibilities, not necessities. A layman may be one of these or the other as he chooses. But he *must be* a theologian. This is not an option with him but a requirement.

1. A Theologian Is One Who Knows About God

Why do we say that a layman must be a theologian? Well, let us first of all realize what a theologian is—that is, an amateur theologian. A theologian is a person who knows about God. A lay theologian is a person who has a true knowledge of God which he understands in nontechnical, nonprofessional, nonacademic terms. However, such a person is truly a theologian.

Is it not clear why a layman must necessarily be a theologian? Is there anyone, layman or otherwise,

who does not need to know God? Does the Scripture
not say, "This is life eternal, that they might know
thee the only true God, and Jesus Christ, whom thou
has sent" (John 17:3)? It is, then, no mere option
with a layman whether he will be a theologian or not,
whether he will have eternal life or not; it is no
option with him whether he will know God or not.
The knowledge of God is necessary to eternal life.
And if eternal life is necessary for every man, then
theology is also necessary for every man.

If a theologian is a person who knows God, then
by reverse reasoning a person who is not a theologian
does not know God. There is no shame in a layman's
being told that he does not know carpentry, or plumb-
ing, or medicine, or law, or teaching, or the ways of a
housewife; but there surely is the greatest of shame
in a layman's being told that he does not know God.
Furthermore, there is more than shame; there is very
great danger. The Scripture says that to live apart
from God is death. And just as the text quoted says
it is life eternal to know God and Christ, another passage in the same book says that they who do not believe in Jesus shall not see life and, furthermore, the
wrath of God abides upon them: "He that believeth
on the Son hath everlasting life: and he that believeth
not the Son shall not see life; but the wrath of God
abideth on him" (John 3:36).

"Well," the layman may say, "look here, you've
slipped in a new term on us. That last passage talks

about faith and not knowledge. It says except a person 'believe' in the Son. It does not say anything there about 'knowing' Jesus." That is true, the passage does not use the word "know." It does speak about "belief" or "faith" rather than "knowledge" or "reason." But have you ever believed in somebody or something about which you knew nothing? Is it possible to have faith in Christ unless we know who Christ is? Is it not clear, therefore, that this passage, though it does not state expressly the necessity of the knowledge of Christ, certainly states it implicitly? So we say that if a person does not have a knowledge of God and Christ it is not only a shame but a peril to his soul, not only in this life but in the eternity which begins at death.

II. Everyman May Be a Theologian Without Being Saved!

"But," the layman exclaims, "do you mean to tell me that if I do not have the knowledge of God I shall perish, and that if I do have the knowledge of God I will live forever? Do you mean to tell me that if I am a lay theologian all is well with my soul, whereas if I am not I am doomed forever?" No, we have not said exactly that. Let me call your attention to what we did actually say, and then let me add a comment relevant to one of your questions. We did say that without knowledge of God there is no eternal life, but only eternal death. That is true. And we did say that if we do not know God and Christ we will perish.

That is true. However, it needs to be brought out now that there is knowledge and knowledge. The knowledge of which the Scripture speaks so approvingly we may call "saving knowledge." But we gather from other passages of Scripture which we have not yet cited that there is also a false knowledge which, far from being saving knowledge, is actually damning knowledge. But it seems to me we are now ready for a closer consideration of this theme. Let me, therefore, lay down this statement and devote the rest of this chapter to demonstrating it. The statement is this: A layman may have knowledge of God and not be saved, but he can never be saved without knowledge of God.

There is much to show that a layman may have theology without having salvation. For one thing, the Bible says in many places that frequently persons have a knowledge about God but do not know God. Thus, for example, the Scripture exhorts us to be not only hearers of the Word but doers also (cf. James 1:22).

This implies that it is possible to hear, or learn, or know, without doing. It goes on to tell us that only the doing of the Word is profitable, again carrying the implication that persons may hear the Word and understand it without actually doing it and therefore without being profitable.

Again, Paul speaks in Romans of those who hold the truth in unrighteousness (1:18). That is the same as to say that some persons know God (and indeed in this very context Paul does speak of knowing God) and yet do not worship Him nor are they being saved by Him. So we learn that while their knowledge is sufficient to condemn them, they are not saved by it.

In the parable of the sower and the seed recorded in Matthew 13, our Lord tells of differing responses to the presentation of the gospel. While the wayside soil represents those persons who seem virtually not to hear what is preached, or not to learn what they are taught, still the other two types of useless soil represent persons who do hear and do understand but who nevertheless do not bring forth fruit. Thus the shallow, rocky soil does represent a person who receives the Word, as Jesus says. He receives it with gladness and even seems to respond favorably to it for a while. But when he is beset by difficulties he repudiates the knowledge which he does have. So we see in his case an individual who knows but does not do, who understands the way of salvation but does not attain to salvation. The thorny soil represents a person who understands and apparently even very deliberately understands and accepts the message but whose knowledge is crushed out in the subsequent contest between that message and his lusts, which are represented by thorns in the soil. But there can be no doubt that he not only has knowledge but deep and penetrating and not merely superficial knowledge. Nonetheless, his knowledge is choked out and the man does not obtain to salvation.

There are many other instances of the possibility of knowing the truth without being saved. But we will take one, that of the Pharisees, and use it as our prime exhibit. The layman will immediately say, "Ah, but the Pharisees were religious teachers and cannot fairly be called laymen." This we admit. But we will also go on to insist that our point is certified all the more by the fact that the Pharisees, as professional theologians, had even greater knowledge than laymen could be expected to have—and yet the Pharisees perished. Remember, we are attempting to show that it is possible to have theological knowledge without being saved. If we can show that one who is regarded as a professional (who has far more religious knowledge than a layman may be expected to have) may yet perish, how much more evident is it that any knowledge that a layman can reasonably be expected to obtain can by no means guarantee his salvation. Jesus approved of the Pharisees in many ways because they attempted to honor Moses' law—and often did—and teach his precepts to the people. However, they came under Christ's withering indictment, "Woe unto you Pharisees, hypocrites," so often that we are led to believe that as a class these highly knowledgeable individuals were not practitioners of their science and therefore were doomed to condemnation. Jesus said to them, "How can you escape the damnation of hell?" (Matt. 23:33).

III. Everyman Cannot Be Saved Without Being a Theologian

If the above is enough to indicate that persons may have divine knowledge without being saved, let us go on to indicate the still more pertinent truth—that no one can be saved without the knowledge of divine truth or theology. This is stated very explicitly in Romans 10:17. Here Paul says, "Faith cometh by hearing." That is as much as to affirm that there can be no belief except first the Word of the gospel is proclaimed. The context of this explicit statement confirms that implication. It is a missionary context in which Paul is urging Christians to take the gospel to the world, reminding them that if they do not do so these people cannot be saved—because faith comes by hearing. In I Corinthians we read that it pleased God by the foolishness of preaching to save men. Again, says Paul, "I am not ashamed of the gospel of Christ: for it is the power of God unto salvation" (Rom. 1:16). And, after commanding the disciples to teach whatsoever He had taught them, our Lord Jesus commissioned them to make disciples of all nations (Matt. 28:19-20). That is the same as to say that it is by means of the faithful proclamation of the whole counsel of God that the world is to be discipled to Jesus Christ. Consider again how our Lord prays in His farewell discourse, "Sanctify them through thy truth: thy Word is truth" (John 17:17). In this final prayer for those who were not yet of His fold but who were to come into His fold, our Lord prayed that they might be made holy by means of the Word of God. Though the Spirit of God was to be given anew as soon as Christ went to Heaven, even the Holy Spirit was not to sanctify except by means of the Word of God. So that while the letter of the Word may be devoid of the Spirit and therefore futile, the Spirit does not work savingly apart from the Word. The Word is called "the sword of the Spirit" (Eph. 6:17). Again, in II Thessalonians 2:13 we read, "God hath from the beginning chosen you to salvation through sanctification of the Spirit and belief of the truth." There we are told very plainly that even the eternal predestination of God is accomplished by the instrumentality of truth. People are not brought to life whether they know or do not know. They are not given salvation whether they believe the truth or not. On the contrary, God chose them to salvation through "belief of the truth."

The Scripture abounds in so many passages which indicate this same truth that it seems to be laboring the matter unduly to add any further discussion of this emphatic point of the Bible. We may safely conclude that though men may know the truth and not be saved, they cannot be saved except they know the truth.

My dear laymen, laymen must be theologians. No, they need not be professional theologians. They need not study Greek and Hebrew. They need not necessarily be able to teach other people. But they must be theologians. That is, they must know God. They must have sound knowledge about God. They may not excuse themselves from having clear and correct opinions about the Deity on the ground that they are not ordained to full-time church work but have been called to some other service.

The duty to be theologians is common to all of us. The difference at this point between laymen and ministers is a difference not of kind but of degree. It is an error of Rome which teaches that there is a difference of kind between priests and people. With the Bible, the Protestant church teaches that the Bible itself was given not solely to the clergy but to all the people of God. We of the clergy have *greater* obligation, not *sole* obligation. So far as time permits, and to the degree that your obligations to this world allow, in that measure must you be familiar with the truth of God. For that knowledge God will hold you responsible in the day of judgment. While you need not read this book or any other particular book except the Book, the Word of God itself, I hope you will read this book to help you in your study of the Bible and in your gaining a sound knowledge of God. But I remind you that while this book may give you some knowledge of God by means of which you may be saved, this book and no other book (indeed, not even the Bible itself) can save you. This truth of God

must be loved, must be embraced, and must be yielded
to if the person who has saving knowledge is to be
saved by it. One theologian has written that it is not
enough to "understand" but you must also "stand
under." For the truth of God is a Person—a Person
who said "I am the way, the *truth,* and the life"
(John 14:6). A true theologian, therefore, is a person
who knows The Person. Everyman must be a theologian.

CHAPTER II

God's Providence: A Two-edged Sword

ACCORDING TO the Westminster Shorter Catechism, "God's works of providence are, his most holy, wise, powerful preserving and governing all his creatures, and all their actions." This comprehensive statement says that God's providence encompasses *all* and not merely *some* of the acts of His creatures. Such a definition would include big events and trifles as well—good things, but also evil. Does not Jeremiah teach the same doctrine? "Who is he that saith, and it cometh to pass, when the Lord commandeth it not?" (Lam. 3:37). Is Acts 15:18 any different? "Known unto God are all his works from the beginning of the world." If known to God are all His deeds from the beginning, there is nothing not known to Him. Nothing escapes His purposes—not a single hair nor a falling sparrow.

Neither you nor I would be here to discuss providence if Providence had not brought us here—if God had not done His will in the earth. How conscious we are of all the little details on which our lives to this point have turned. I do not know the trifles in your life, but I do know those in my own. Let me mention one. If a child had dropped a marble one inch more to the left or for some reason I had put my foot one inch more to the right as I once went down a fire escape I would not now, probably, be discussing providence at all.

Not only in your life and mine but in the lives of historic public figures the same significance of detail is apparent. A.H. Strong in his *Systematic Theology* reminds us that Muhammad's life once was suspended by a literal thread. The prophet, fleeing his enemies, hid in a cave across which a spider quickly spun a web. When the pursuers saw it, they were convinced that there was no one in the cave. They went on. Muhammad was spared. His religion today numbers more than three hundred million adherents.

But if trifles are vital parts of divine providence, what of evil? Evil is often vastly significant. The most important event which ever occurred was, in one aspect, horribly evil. The crucifixion of Jesus from the standpoint of the crucifiers was grotesquely wicked. Yet, even though the killing of Christ was atrocity itself, what event was so vital and its effects so beneficial as the death of Christ? If God's providence does not include evil, it does not include the most important event which has ever taken place.

So we say providence is a two-edged sword. It cuts both ways bringing (differently, to be sure, but bringing nonetheless) both the good and the evil. If we deny either, we deny providence. If we deny providence, we deny God. If we deny the benign, we deny the goodness of God. If we deny the evil, we deny the severity of God. The Bible denies neither, but affirms each. "Behold therefore the goodness and severity of God: on them which fell, severity; but toward thee, goodness, if thou continue in his goodness: otherwise thou also shalt be cut off" (Rom. 11:22).

Let us consider then these two aspects of divine providence. But first we examine what we shall call "negative providence."

I. Negative Providence

A. *Definition*

What do we mean by negative providence? Suppose we begin with the comedian Ed Wynn's definition based on a slight alteration of some famous lines:

"There is a destiny that shapes our ends rough;
Hew them how we may."

This is negative enough, but is it providence? No, this is Greek fatalism rather than Christian providence. Why? Because human behavior is disregarded. "Hew them how we may"—that makes no difference. Compare, for an example of this type of thinking, the great Greek tragedian Sophocles' *Oedipus Rex*. This king, Oedipus, is destined to kill his father and marry his mother. No matter how innocent of either he may try to be, he unknowingly and inevitably does both. Though he consciously strives to avoid these sins, he does them nonetheless and is held guilty for them. So his mother commits suicide, and he gouges out his eyes and goes into solitary and hopeless exile.

The certainty of the end is present in this tragic definition of negative providence. It also contains the element of human activity. In the Wynn satire the man "hews"; in Sophocles' tragedy Oedipus does all in his power to avoid fate. Neither actor is a puppet. Each one strives, though to no avail. But, what is lacking in these two accounts? It is the connection between the end and the means. There is *no* connection between end and means; between destiny and striving. The end comes to pass regardless of striving; indeed, it comes in spite of striving against it. The destiny shapes ends rough, hew them how we may— that is, though we hew to the moral line in an endeavor to make our destiny smooth, it remains rough. Oedipus is essentially a moral person, generally admired by his family and subjects. But all this means nothing, for he is destined to commit the accursed crimes of patricide and incest (and accursed crimes they remain although he intends neither of them).

What a contrast to all this is the negative providence of Scripture! Compare Acts 2:23: "Him, being delivered by the determinate counsel and foreknowledge of God, ye have taken, and by wicked hands have crucified and slain." Judas and others indeed delivered Christ up according to the eternal counsel and foreknowledge of God, but they did so by "wicked hands." Their "hands" were not inactive. They were certainly not opposed to this dread deed. On the contrary, they willfully chose to do the awful deed, for they were denominated "wicked hands." This illustrates the constant Bible teaching about negative providence; namely, that the doers are always voluntary doers, willing actors, guilty men.

Putting the picture together, this is what we find: Negative providence is the divine appointment even. of wicked and calamitous events but not apart from —rather, through—the willing though wicked determinations of men.

B. *Forms of Negative Providence*

1. *External*

Providence applies to the totality of things. Since we are here concerned only with the human creature, we note that providence applies to the total person. The total human person is a composite one. Thomas Aquinas has observed that man, in possessing a spirit, resembles angels; in possessing a body, he resembles animals. Furthermore, in addition to man's having two parts to his personality, body and spirit, he has two periods—time and eternity. Providence relates both to the temporal and to the eternal.

So we consider first that form of negative providence which affects the external, bodily, and temporal aspect of the human personality. Christ referred to temporal providence when He spoke of the hairs of our head being numbered. Both our temporal lives and our environment are part of providence. But the tragic as well as the beneficent elements of the external and temporal are part of providence. For example, Christ said that He must go as it was written of Him, that He must be killed at Jerusalem and that the Shepherd will be smitten, and the like. All of these evil events concerning death are therefore of divine foreordination.

There is a time coming, says the Bible, when God will reveal more fully the displeasure which He now feels. Meanwhile, it appears to the Psalmist as if God is slumbering and needs to be aroused. But God is waiting until the "cup of iniquity" is full. Thus He withheld his judgment upon the Amorites. "But in the fourth generation they shall come hither again: for the iniquity of the Amorites is not yet full" (Gen. 15:16). But though it might seem that God's judgments are delayed, Moses warned the Israelites, "Be sure your sins will find you out" (Num. 32:23). He told them in his farewell address, as well as on other occasions, of the curses which were sure to overtake those who turned away from Jehovah.

We have impressive illustrations of this negative providence pertaining to the externals here and now. Consider, for example, the fall of Jerusalem. Christ was crucified and nothing happened—then. Later, in the lifetime of the same generation, the city was besieged, civil war, famine, butchery, and indescribable suffering took place. Mothers devoured their own children as the wrath of God came upon the city that crucified His Son.

Nor are visitations of wrath only in the form of military woes and desolations. Roger Babson once made an investigation of bankruptcies in the United States during a certain number of years. Some of these business collapses were traceable to lack of competence—a few. The majority were owing to lack of integrity and honesty.

The eminent historian of the American scene, Charles Beard, said that one of the lessons he learned from his studies was that the mills of the gods grind slowly but they grind exceeding fine. Still another scholar said in a class that if he were intimately familiar with the condition of a community he could predict within a hundred years the date of its downfall. Then he revised that statement claiming that he could predict the downfall within the space of ten years.

Not only do the scholars recognize the temporal judgments which come on mankind and the brimstone which is scattered over all the possessions of wicked men but even the man on the street knows it and sometimes even jokes about it. For example, I used to go bowling with my church people on Thursday nights. Occasionally I would bowl the ball in the corner properly and it would move over to center as it ought and a strike appeared certain. I would start to walk back to the bench. But alas all the pins would

not fall down—the two farthest apart still stood! My
men should have said: "You were robbed, pastor."
"You should have had a strike, pastor." "Too bad,
pastor." What they did say was: "You don't live right,
pastor!"

2. *Internal*

"Your sins will find you out," said Moses. However,
not all visitation is upon the bodies of sinners; it
comes upon the souls also. God may wait to pour out
wrath upon the external world until the cup of iniquity is full, but apparently He pours out this invisible cup on the soul as soon as it sins. He may seem
to slumber as He delays external punishment, but not
so in the administration of internal suffering. A person may sin and retribution upon his body not be
forthcoming, but his conscience is immediately af-
flicted. He may, indeed, get away *with* it; he never
gets away *from* it. "The wicked flee when no man
pursueth"; that is, their consciences are alarmed
when there is no outward apprehension. "God is
angry with the wicked every day" (Ps. 7:11). That is,
though the wicked prosper outwardly as the green bay
tree, he is inwardly blighted. The wicked is as the
surging of the sea (Isa. 57:20). That is, however
tranquil his situation may appear to be, he has no
true peace within. John Calvin says the sinner sometimes has tranquility because he is too "thick" to
understand the judgment of God against him. But

he is not tranquil about his tranquility. That is, he is disturbed about his peace of mind. There is no rest for the wicked one even when they are resting because they still vaguely and apprehensively wonder whether they should rest, whether all *is* well with their soul.

II. Positive Providence

A. Definition

When considering the definition of negative providence we used Ed Wynn's comic parody of the poet. Now, considering positive providence, we consider the poet himself:

> "There is a destiny which shapes our ends
> Rough hew them though we may."

The "rough hew" needs explanation. If the poet means "sin as we please," if he suggests that a positive providence comes about irrespective of our behavior, if things are going to work out well although we always behave badly—then he errs in the opposite direction. Just as there is no destiny that shapes our ends rough, hew them how we may, neither is there any destiny which shapes our ends well, hew them how we may. The shaping and the hewing are integrally related. God shapes as we hew; we hew as God shapes. So, then, the definition of positive providence is: The divine appointment of good and beneficial events but not apart from (rather, through) the willing determinations of men.

B. *Forms of Positive Providence*

1. *External*

"And we know that all things work together for good to them that love God, to them who are the called according to his purpose" (Rom. 8:28). That includes external and temporal events as well as the internal and eternal. "Wherein ye greatly rejoice, though now for a season, if need be, ye are in heaviness through manifold temptations: That the trial of your faith, being much more precious than of gold that perisheth, though it be tried with fire, might be found unto praise and honor and glory at the appearing of Jesus Christ" (I Peter 1:6-7). "We are accounted as sheep for the slaughter," but nothing "shall be able to separate us from the love of God, which is in Christ Jesus our Lord" (Rom. 8:36, 39). "In the world ye shall have tribulation: but be of good cheer; I have overcome the world" (John 16:33). "Therefore being justified by faith, we have peace with God through our Lord Jesus Christ: by whom also we have access by faith into this grace wherein we stand, and rejoice in hope of the glory of God. And not only so, but we glory in tribulations also: knowing that tribulation worketh patience" (Rom. 5:1-3). So these adversities are transformed by divine grace and wisdom into blessings. The same event which is negative providence for the wicked is positive providence for the children of God. The meek, says Jesus, shall inherit the *earth*. Righteousness exalts a *nation*. The wicked may appear to prosper, but their way perishes while he who meditates on the law of God day and night shall be like a tree planted by the rivers of waters (Ps. 1:2).

Honesty may work a temporary temporal disadvantage, but in the long run, even in this evil world, honesty pays. Crime may be a temporary temporal advantage, but in the long run, even in this evil world, crime does not pay. They that take the sword shall perish with the sword while the peacemakers shall be called, even in this world, "the children of God."

2. *Internal*

If there is no rest for the wicked even in this world, there is rest for the righteous even in this world. They have peace with God, access to grace, hope of glory. For them to live is Christ and to die is gain only because they will have still more of Christ. For the Christian it is: all this and Heaven too.

Note how this internal joy transforms even the temporal bodily pain to which Christians are subject in this life. A former president of Colgate University was stricken and suffered almost incessantly. His son could not refrain from saying: "Father, I wish I could bear some of your pain for you." "Son," the sufferer replied, "I do not have a pain to spare." A woman in a congregation where this story was told said: "That

man must never have had gall bladder trouble!"
Seriously, a Christian has *no* pain to spare.

What shall it be for you? A positive or negative
providence? Do you wish divine destiny to shape
things rough or smooth? In this world and that which
is to come?

Remember that providence is not fatalism. Your
hewing is related to God's shaping. God's shaping is
related to your hewing.

CHAPTER III

Sin Makes No Racial Distinctions

S PEAKING OF GOD'S PROVIDENCE we noticed sin incidentally. We now bring it into focus. One cannot think of God's holy ways without thinking of our
unholy ones. We cannot think of ourselves without
thinking of our sin. Sin is the most important conviction any man can have. It is a bad theology which
thinks man good. Any good theology must start with
man as bad.

In the opening verses of chapter two of Ephesians,
Paul describes unconverted persons by many different
expressions. They are called "dead through trespasses
and sins"; they are seen as walking in the "course of
this world," walking "according to the prince of the
power of the air," fulfilling "the lusts of the flesh and
of the mind," and "by nature" they are "children of
wrath." The former terms refer to the expressions of
their character. The last expression, "children of
wrath," is the root cause of their character. It is because the unconverted or unquickened person is by
nature a child of wrath that he is dead in trespasses
and sin and walks according to the will of the world,
the devil, and the flesh. These evil works reveal him

as naturally liable to "wrath" —the wrath of God,
His abiding fury. That is, the unconverted person—
whoever he may be—is, by nature, doomed to destruction, for sin is no respecter of persons. Be he a Gen-
tile, like those to whom Paul wrote, or a Jew, like
Paul himself, he is a child of wrath. Sin makes no
racial distinctions.

I. Sin No Respecter of Persons

All people, in and out of the church, are by nature
children of wrath. Paul begins his description of the
unconverted by referring to the Gentiles, the Ephesians, who were outside the commonwealth of Israel,
strangers to the promises of God, etc. However, before he finishes his description, he includes Israel as
well in the indictment, saying: "Among whom also
we [we Israelites also] had our conversation in the
times past in the lusts of our flesh, fulfilling the desires of the flesh and of the mind; and were by nature
the children of wrath, even as others." Paul thereby
teaches that although Israelites had received circum-
cision, which was "the seal of righteousness by faith,"
they were not thereby changed in nature. Because
they had been engrafted into the visible church, they
were not thereby necessarily engrafted into the invisible body of Christ. They, just like the Gentiles
("pagans") whom they despised as outside the law,
needed to be born again. Though they were heirs of
the promises, they still remained by nature children of

wrath, even as the others. It was a Jew—and a Jewish ruler at that (Nicodemus) —to whom Jesus had said: "Ye must be born again" (John 3:3) .

II. *Proof That Sin Is No Respecter of Persons*

A. *General Bible Teaching*

Note how this teaching of Ephesians is corroborated everywhere in Scripture. David says in Psalm 51: "I was shapen in iniquity; and in sin did my mother conceive me." In Psalm 58:3 we read: "The wicked are estranged from the womb; they go astray as soon as they be born, speaking lies." Eliphaz, one of Job's three friends, is very emphatic: "What is man, that he should clean? and he which is born of a woman, that he should be righteous? Behold, he putteth no trust in his saints: yea, the heavens are not clean in his sight. How much more abominable and filthy is man, which drinketh iniquity like water?" (Job 15: 14-16) . In 14:4 Job asks, "Who can bring a clean thing out of an unclean?" Job is speaking here expressly of man being born of a woman, as spoken of in verse 1. This is given as a reason for man's not being clean. That is, being a human creature, proceeding by ordinary generation, man is naturally polluted.

B. *"Man" Used Synonymously with "Sinner"*

The Bible sees man so constantly and universally associated with sin that it virtually uses the term "man" as synoymous with "sin." "Cursed is he that

trusteth in man," said the Lord in Jeremiah 17:5.
Christ said to Peter, "Get thee behind me, Satan. . . .
for thou savorest not the things that be of God, but
those that be of men" (Matt. 16:23). This plainly
signifies that to be carnal and vain—opposite to what
is spiritual and divine—is what properly belongs to
men in their present sinful state. Compare also I Corinthians 3:3; I Peter 4:2; Job 15:6.

C. *Man More Destructive than Animals*

That man is more wicked and destructive than even
voracious and wild animals is clear from a somber
remark of our Lord. When He sent forth his disciples
into the world, to bear witness of Him, He said: "Behold, I send you forth as sheep in the midst of wolves:
. . . but beware of men." It was as if He said, "I send
you forth as sheep among wolves. But why do I say
wolves? I send you forth into the wide world of men,
that are far more dangerous than wolves." Jonathan
Edwards was justified in saying: "There is no one
lust in the heart of the devil that is not in the heart of
man. Natural men are in the image of the devil. The
image of God is rased out and the image of the devil
is stamped upon them."[1]

One writer tells of a Christian who in prayer cited
the words of Jeremiah, "The heart is deceitful and
desperately wicked," and then continued by saying:
"O Lord, Thou knowest we no longer accept this

[1]"Natural Men in a Dreadful Condition," *Works*, VIII, 10.

interpretation." This amounts to saying that we no longer accept the Bible's interpretation of sin. But for us to reject the verdict of the Word of God about sin is a dreadful act of sin, is it not? So if we deny the sin which the Bible says is in our hearts, we prove that it is there, do we not? Perhaps the very best proof of the sin of our hearts is that we deny the sin of our hearts.

In or out of the church, then, the unconverted person's liability to eternal destruction is not occasioned by his environment but by his inherited nature. "We are by nature children of wrath." It is not by what we do that we are children of wrath, but by what we are. We do not become children of wrath by doing evil things, but we do evil things because we are children of wrath. Of course, doing evil makes us more and more the children of wrath. As Christ said, the proselytes of the Pharisees became twofold more the children of Hell than they (Matt. 23:15). Not by environment are we the children of wrath, but by nature. It is our nature which makes our environment evil and not our environment which makes our natures evil. This is the startling thing that the inspired Apostle taught in Ephesians 2:3.

Reinhold Niebuhr, America's distinguished neo-orthodox theologian, lectured to the students and faculty of Harvard Divinity School in 1940. He was discussing original sin and gave this domestic illustration. His son, who was then seven, had been in a neighborhood brawl. Niebuhr was inclined to finish what the boys had begun, but the maid interceded. "Professor Niebuhr," she said, "it is not your son's fault. It's the company he keeps." The father replied: "It is not the company he keeps. It is his own little black heart."

D. *Even Infants Are Polluted*

What shows the iniquity of man most clearly of all is that infants themselves are contaminated with sin. Before babies learn how to think or speak or act responsibly they are by nature children of wrath. The Bible shows this first of all inferentially. That is, it teaches clearly that the wages of sin is death. Where there is no sin, there would be no death. If there were no sin, there would be no suffering. Yet babies both suffer and die. Sometimes they suffer dreadfully and sometimes they die in agony. "Therefore," said John Wesley, "children themselves are not innocent before God. They suffer, therefore they deserve to suffer." Or as the Lutheran theologian Sohnius puts it: "Since infants die, as universal experience teaches, it is evident that they must be chargeable with sin; for Paul clearly represents sin as the cause of death—of the death of all men. 'For the wages of sin is death.' " John Calvin says: "We are by nature the children of wrath. But God does not condemn the innocent. Therefore, . . . " And so Calvin argues that God's calling our natures guiltily corrupt proves that we are corrupt and, at the same time, responsible for our native corruption.

Some moderns have jumped to the conclusion that there is no necessary connection between sin and suffering and death. This they do because our Lord has told us there is no necessary connection between a particular sin and a particular suffering. A calamity coming upon a particular person is no proof that the person is a greater sinner than one on whom that particular calamity did not come. But Chirst nowhere says that suffering is unconnected with sin, or that there would be death where there was no sin.

Continuing with the sinfulness of infants, we call attention to the divinely commanded execution of some Midianite children, mentioned in Numbers 31: 17. Moses there commanded the Israelites to slay all of the male children, as Saul was commanded on a later occasion to slay all the infants of the Amalekites, I Samuel 15:3. In Psalm 137:9 we read: "Happy shall he be, that taketh and dasheth thy little ones against the stones." Edwards, in his *Great Christian Doctrine of Original Sin,* says: "I proceed to take notice of something remarkable concerning the destruction of Jerusalem, represented in Ezek. 9, when command was given [to them that had charge over the city] to destroy the inhabitants, ver. 1-8. And this reason is given for it, that their iniquity required it, and it was a just recompense of their sin (ver. 9, 10). God, at the same time, was most particular and exact in his

care, that such as had proved by their behavior, that
they were not partakers in the abominations of the
city, should by no means be involved in the slaughter.
Command was given to the angel to go through the
city, and set a mark upon their foreheads, and the de-
stroying angel had a strict charge not to come near any
man, on whom was the mark; yet the infants were not
marked nor a word said of sparing them: on the contrary, infants were expressly mentioned as those that
should be utterly destroyed, without pity (ver. 5, 6).
'Go through the city and smite: let not your eye spare,
neither have ye pity. Slay utterly old and *young*, both
maids and *little children*; but come not near any man
upon whom is the mark. ' " Sodom would have been
spared by God if there had been ten righteous; since
there must have been ten infants, these could not have
been righteous. We read in Proverbs 22:15: "Foolishness is bound in the heart of a child; but the rod of
correction shall drive it far from him." Matthew 18:
11 says that the Son of man came "to save that which is
lost." If, therefore, children who die are saved, as
many believe, it is from a lost condition by nature!

E. *Inevitability of Punishment*

Not only do the above passages teach us that any
unconverted person is exposed to wrath but they also
teach that it is absolutely certain to come upon him.
The expression "children of wrath" was a Hebrew
idiom. It meant that the person so described was

inevitably liable to wrath. It was an idiomatic way of saying what Paul says more conventionally in Romans 9. There he speaks of "vessels of wrath fitted to destruction." In Deuteronomy 25:2 the expression "son of stripes" is used to signify one who is to be beaten. In II Samuel 12:5, the expression "son of death" is used of one who is certain to die. We remember that Christ referred to Judas as the "son of perdition," the heir of Hell, the one certain to receive that dread destiny. In Ephesians 2:2 Paul shows that the unconverted person is already under the "prince of the power of the air." Every soul is the habitation of unclean spirits, precisely because by nature he is a child of wrath.

So we have seen from the Ephesians text, from other statements of Scripture, from biblical references to man as virtually synonymous with sinner and worse than an animal and more like a devil, from the lost condition even of babies, and from the inevitability of punishment, that the unconverted are by nature— not by environment, and without respect to persons or distinction of race—children of wrath.

III. Application of the Universality of Sin

Let us now apply this doctrine to ourselves. First, let me apply it to myself. This means that, though I am a minister of the gospel, I am by nature a child of wrath. Even Paul, the greatest of ministers and apostles, included himself. "We also," he said. No privilege or opportunity can blind us to this sober fact. Indeed, a true minister is one who preaches as a dying man to dying men, telling them of a Saviour who can save both him and them.

Second, as professing Christians we need to take warning. We have already shown that we, too, are "by nature children of wrath even as the rest." Let us not say to ourselves, "Abraham is our father." Let us not say we are Presbyterians, Lutherans, Baptists. Let us not say that we come to church regularly and give our tithes and teach our class and visit the sick. We are by nature children of wrath, just like the rest of this perishing world. If we have a hope of salvation, it must be on some other basis than what we are. By nature we are lost. Let us not say, "Lord, I thank thee that I am not like other men. I am not like people who play golf on Sunday afternoons, or people who give less than a nickel a week to charity, or people who read foul novels and tell dirty stories." We are by nature children of wrath just like the rest. There is no hope for you, no matter what you join or what you do or what you say unless you acknowledge that you are in yourself reeking with corruption and in a lost condition by nature, a dwelling place for the devil, an enemy of God, a hypocrite, and a criminal. What has made the matter worse is that you have thought well of yourself. You resent having anyone, even God, calling you names because you consider yourself a decent person, one who dwells among decent people.

But the Bible tells you, you are no saint. You must recognize yourself to be a sinner by birth and by nature (Luke 18:13-14). Only one who recognizes that he is a sinner can ever be a saint. Sinners deny that they are sinners—for the sin of lying is part of their sin. Saints admit that they are sinners by nature, for as saints they now tell the truth.

Third, those outside the church need to be warned. Professing Christians are presumably repentant (though by no means necessarily so, as we have previously seen). Those outside the church are presumably impenitent (though there may be very rare exceptions). Faith comes by hearing, and hearing by the Word of God (Rom. 10:17). Generally, those outside the church do not hear the Word of God, by which faith and salvation comes. That is, they do not hear it unless you tell them. Unless they hear it, they who —like you—are by nature children of wrath will most certainly perish under the judgment of God. The wrath of God is upon them now. His fury burns hot against them. Their life hangs by a thin thread, and when that thread is broken, they will go to their everlasting home of suffering. How shall they hear without a preacher? You, as a Christian, are their preacher. Do not worry only about what will happen to people who never hear the gospel. Worry about what will

happen to you if you never tell them the gospel.
They will perish, but you will be held responsible by
God for your failure to give them the gospel. There
is positively no way by which they can escape the
wrath which is to come and that which now is, except
through the only name given under Heaven whereby
men may be saved—the name of Jesus. You have that
name. If you truly believe in it and are trusting in
Christ's grace for your salvation, you will most certainly try, as opportunity affords, to win some. "Knowing the terror of the Lord, we persuade men," said
Paul. And, knowing the love of the Lord, we should
persuade men, too. "We thus judge, that if one died
for all, then were all dead: and that he died for all,
that they which live should no longer live unto themselves, but unto him which died for them, and rose
again" (II Cor. 5:14-15). The love of Christ constrains men; the terror of Christ constrains men.

Fourth, nothing less than a change of nature is
needed. If we are by nature children of wrath we can
only become children of grace by new birth. When
we read that a very religious man of great influence
and reputation came to Jesus and was told, "Except a
man be born again, he cannot see [or enter] the kingdom of God," we realize that a radical change is necessary. This religious man had to be born from above;
he had to be born again. He had to be given a new
nature. He had to be born twice. He had to have a
radical transformation of soul. The ruling disposition

of his life had to be changed. Until that time, there was no hope for him. He was by nature a child of wrath just like the rest. He was a perishing sinner. Every moment that he lived, he was odious to God. Every moment that he continued his impenitent way, he was storing up wrath against the day of wrath. Every moment that he lived, he was making the fires of Hell that much hotter. The time would come when he would wish that he had never lived a happy moment longer. The time would come when he would wish that he had never been born. It would be better for that man if he had never been born, or if a millstone had been tied about his neck and he were cast into the sea. Being a child of wrath is as dreadful as being a child of glory is wonderful.

CHAPTER IV

Jesus Christ: The God-Man

WE HAD A VERY INTERESTING PROFESSOR at Harvard University who used to attempt to introduce Christ to his classes. In attendance, he would have, in addition to the divinity school men, a number of the regular university students. The latter were often totally ignorant of Christ. This fact, far from dismaying the professor, rather pleased him; for from these students he got what he liked to call "the virgin reaction" to Jesus. The theological students, having been acquainted with Jesus before, could only afford the philosophy of the second glance. But Dr. H. J. Cadbury, who himself had studied the texts hundreds of times, could always learn something from those who would give the fresh response of the newly introduced. Let us attempt to put ourselves in the position of these students and try to experience the initial response to Jesus Christ.

I. *The Humanity of Christ*

When we read the accounts of Jesus we instinctively recognize Him as the perfect man. Matthew describes One whom we see to be the ideal Jew; Mark, the ideal Roman; John, the ideal Son of God; and Luke, the universal ideal who is every man's ideal and God's as well. Furthermore, every man who approaches Christ seems to feel the same thing—He is the ideal of that man. To the artist Christ is the One altogether lovely. To the educator He is the master teacher. To the philosopher He is the wisdom of God. To the lonely, He is a brother; to the sorrowful, a comforter; and to the bereaved, the resurrection and the life. To the sinner, He is the Lamb of God that takes away the sin of the world.

"No one," says Watson, "has yet discovered the word Jesus ought to have said, none suggested the better word he might have said. No action of his has shocked our moral sense. None has fallen short of the ideal. He is full of surprises, but they are all the surprises of perfection. You are never amazed one day by his greatness, the next by his littleness. You are quite amazed that he is incomparably better than you could have expected. He is tender without being weak, strong without being coarse, lowly without being servile. He has conviction without intolerance, enthusiasm without fanaticism, holiness without Pharisaism, passion without prejudice. This man alone never made a false step, never struck a jarring note. His life alone moved on those high levels where local limitations are transcended and the absolute Law of Moral Beauty prevails. It was life at its Highest."

The virgin reaction of the world to Jesus Christ is, then, this: He is the ideal, the perfect man; the moral paragon of the race. I do not wish to gloss over the fact that not absolutely everyone has agreed with this verdict. I know that George Bernard Shaw spoke of a time in Christ's life when, as he said, Christ was not a Christian. I know that some have thought that Socrates died more nobly than Jesus; that others believe Christ to have been surpassed. But the overwhelming testimony of the world is to the perfection, the incomparable perfection, of Jesus of Nazareth. These few exceptions could be easily shown to rest on fundamental misconceptions of certain things which Jesus said or did. Moreover, those who do take exception usually think that some imagined fault is a failure of Christ to be, as G. B. Shaw said, a Christian! It is evident that they know of no higher standard by which to test Christ than the standard of Christ Himself.

II. The Deity of Christ

But now we find ourselves in an extraordinary situation. If we admit, as the world does, that Christ is the perfect man, we must then admit that He is also God! Why, you ask, if we acknowledge Christ to be the perfect man, must we then acknowledge Him to be God also? Is there not a great difference between man and God—even between perfect man and God? Why should the admission of the one require the admission of the other? Why must the perfect man be God? For this reason: Because the perfect man *says* he is God. And if He is not God, then neither could He be a perfect man. We despise Father Divine, as a man, for claiming to be God when we know that he is not. If Jesus Christ is not God, we must despise Him also, for He claims far more clearly than Father Divine that He is God. We must, therefore, either worship Christ as God, or despise or pity Him as man.

A. *His own Claim to Deity*

Just a minute, you say, what proof do we have that Jesus Christ ever claimed that He actually is God? My answer is that we have overwhelming evidence that He entertained this high opinion of Himself. This, for example, is what He says of Himself:

"I and my Father are one" (John 10:30).

"No man cometh to the Father, but by me" (John 14:6).

"He that hath seen me hath seen the Father" (John 14:9).

"Before Abraham was, I am" (John 8:58).

"I adjure thee by the living God, that thou tell us whether thou be the Christ, the Son of God," the high priest asked. "Thou hast said," was Christ's reply (Matt. 26:63-64).

"Baptize," He commanded, "in the name of the Father, and of the Son, and of the Holy Ghost" (Matt. 28:19).

"Whom do ye say that I am?" He asked His disciples. "Thou art the Christ, the Son of the living God," Peter replied (Matt. 16:16).

"Blessed art thou, Simon Bar-jona: for flesh and blood hath not revealed it unto thee, but my Father which is in heaven," He said (Matt. 16: 17).

Well, you say, is this not a characteristic way for religious teachers to speak? Do not all of them make grandiose statements? It is true that Bronson Alcott once said to a friend, "Today I feel that I could say, as Christ did, 'I and the Father are one!'" "Yes," the other replied, "but the difference is this: Christ got the world to believe Him."

The significant thing is this: not one recognized religious leader in the history of the world has ever laid claim to being God—except Jesus. Moses did not. Paul was horrified when people tried to worship him. Muhammad insisted that he was merely a prophet of Allah. Buddha did not even believe in the existence of a personal God, and Confucius was skeptical. Zoroaster was a worshiper, but he was not worshiped. We repeat—of the recognized religious leaders of all time, Jesus of Nazareth—and Jesus of Nazareth alone—claimed to be eternal God.

Not only did Jesus on various occasions definitely affirm His deity but it is perhaps more telling still that He always assumed it. Take, for example, the

Sermon on the Mount. This is regarded as predominantly moral instruction. No heavy theology here, they say. This is Christ telling us what we are to do; not what we are to believe about Him. It is true that He does not directly claim to be God in this passage. Indirectly, however, He says a great deal about Himself and lays impressive incidental claim to His divinity.

Note these six distinct pointers to His supernatural being in this one sermon on Christian morality (Matt. 5-7). First, He says with absolute authority who shall and who shall not inherit the kingdom of God (the beatitudes). If I, for example, said anything like that, on my own authority, you would smile pityingly or frown. Second, He said that His disciples would be hated and suffer persecution for His sake. Suppose that I said that Martin Luther suffered for my sake, what would you think about me? Third, "but I say unto you" is a constant refrain through this sermon, by which Christ assumes His right to speak with the authority of the Word of God on which He was commenting. Fourth, He says that in the last judgment people will say to Him, "Lord, Lord"; but "then I will profess unto them, I never knew you: depart from me, ye that work iniquity." Fifth, the sermon concludes with the parable of the two houses, one built on sand and the other on a rock; one to fall and one to stand. And what is this rock? His teaching. Finally, the people sensed the supreme dignity of this person who had taught them, for they observed that "he taught them as one having authority, and not as the scribes."

B. *Contemporaries Affirm Christ's Deity*

What did Jesus' contemporaries think of Him? "Behold the man," said Pilate. "Truly this was the Son of God," said the centurion who watched Him die. "Never man so spake," the people said. "Behold the Lamb of God," was the testimony of John the Baptist, whom all men recognized as a prophet. "My Lord, and my God," said doubting Thomas. When Jesus asked His disciples who they thought He was, Peter, standing near Caesarea Philippi, a city built in honor of Caesar who was claiming divine honors, and not far from the grotto to Pan, the god of nature whom many worshiped, said: "Thou art the Christ, the Son of the living God." John said of Him, "We beheld his glory, the glory as of the only begotten of the Father, full of grace and truth." And Paul adored Him with a most abundant variety of expressions as his great God and Saviour, Jesus Christ. For example, he uses the expression, "unsearchable riches of Christ," and other expressions concerning Christ's riches in his epistles. What does Paul mean by the "unsearchable riches of Christ"? That is the very point. It is impossible to put enough meaning into the expression to do justice to the feeling of the Apostle. Rendell Harris, attempting to translate this expression in Ephesians 3:8, threw up his hands in despair and cried: "The unexplorable wealth of Christ!"

C. Influence of Christ Implies His Deity

What of the influence of Jesus Christ on the succeeding centuries? Shortly before His death, He said: "Believe me for the very works' sake. Verily, verily, I say unto you, He that believeth on me, the works that I do shall he do also; and greater works than these shall he do" (John 14:11b-12). These were very ordinary men to whom Christ—admittedly the most extraordinary person ever to appear in human history—said that they should do greater works than He had done. A strange prediction that was, and stranger still that it has been fulfilled. Yet even stranger still is how it has been fulfilled.

When Christ uttered this prophecy, infanticide was a common thing. Quintillian and others regarded it as a beautiful custom to abandon infants. It was the followers of Jesus, to whom Jesus had said, "Suffer the little children to come unto me, and forbid them not," who put an end to this "beautiful custom." Clement, Origen, Tertullian, the fathers of the church, exposed the horror of infanticide. And the weakest of all creatures, the human infant, became the best protected of all, as the followers of Jesus continued to much greater lengths the emancipation of childhood. As James Stalker has written:

Christ converted the home into a church, and parents into His ministers; and it may be doubted whether He has not by this means won to Himself as many disciples in the course of the Christian ages as even by the institution of the church itself.

Murder for pleasure was eradicated by the disciples of Christ. When Jesus uttered the promise about "greater works," the Romans regarded gladiatorial combats as the choicest of amusements. The bloodier the battle of condemned slaves or captives the rarer the diversion. Telemachus, who leaped into the arena in an attempt to separate the warriors and succeeded only in having himself stoned by an enraged mob of spectators who saw in this man only a mad spoilsport, was, of course, a Christian. He died, but gladiatorial combats were to die with him, as the church was to do greater works in this area than her Founder.

Another example is cannibalism. Of all the atrocious deeds of man against man, the most gruesome is cannibalism. With this practice of degenerate savagery Christ had no personal contact; yet its abolition is the work of those who, in His name, have done greater works than He. When a South Pacific islander told a European mocker of foreign missions that if it had not been for the missionaries he would not be alive to say that he did not believe in missions, he was true to the record. It was through missionaries, a number of whom actually became victims of this hideous practice, that cannibalism has been almost entirely exterminated. Many a soldier in World War II subsequently told of his amazement to find himself welcomed rather than devoured in some remote island where he had been stranded. How glad were such men, who trudged wearily through the jungles with a fear of what the next clearing would reveal, when they saw Christian churches and knew that they were safe. These were the experiences which made missionaries of GI's and produced the now famous "khaki-colored viewpoint." They found the church there, for the disciples were doing greater works than their Lord.

Time would fail us to mention all the *gesta Christi.* Suffice it here to repeat what James Russell Lowell said a century ago, "Show me a place on the face of the earth ten miles square where a man may provide for his children in decency and comfort, where infancy is protected, where age is venerated, where womanhood is honored, and where human life is held in due regard, and I will show you a place where the gospel of Christ has gone and laid the foundation."

III. Conclusion

We are fully aware that to attribute Godhood to any man is a colossal affirmation. It borders on the incredible—the impossible. But when we consider the impression of Christ's perfect humanity, the great claims He made for Himself in the most humble way, the unrestrained adoration and worship of those who knew Him, the miracles associated with Him whose life was a "blaze of miracle," and the constantly recurring miracles of grace which have attended the heralding of His name throughout the world, we propose (if it is difficult to believe that a man was also God) that it is impossible to deny Christ's deity. It is difficult to believe; it is impossible to doubt.

What will you do with Jesus?

NOTE: The above was largely taken from the author's *Reasons For Faith*, published by Harper & Row with their permission. This same volume may be consulted to see how we show that Christ certifies the Bible as the Word of God. In this present volume we are, therefore, merely assuming the authority of Scripture and basing our teaching on it.

CHAPTER V

Atonement: How Jesus Paid It All

1. Christ's Agony

GETHSEMANE was the place of Christ's exquisite torment. Here we see the Man of Sorrows acquainted with grief. Matthew tells us that after the last supper with His apostles He began to be sorrowful. At the supper He had been full of joy. Though the supper represented vividly to Him the death He was to accomplish on the morrow, He was still very happy because He was with His own. His sorrow then was sublimated in a sense of the joy that should follow. Here feasting with Him were the very ones for whom He was to die so that they should be able to feast with him forever. Though the cup was the new testament in His blood, as He told them, He was comforted in the anticipation of eating and drinking again with them in the kingdom of Heaven. "With desire," He had said, "have I desired to eat this passover with you." His desire was fulfilled.

The sorrow of Christ was like that of a soldier about to go into battle—a battle which he knows means suffering and death—who is spending his last night with his family. There is his dear wife and beloved children for whom he would go out to fight and die. So on that last evening the divine Soldier was happy because He was in the presence of those for whom He was soon to die, and surrounded by their love. Christ was not sorrowful then; His own grief was swallowed up in the joy of being with His disciples.

But when the supper was over and they all went out after singing the *Hallel,* the divine Warrior was left with His thoughts about the dread battle soon to be waged in order that He might save those with whom He had so happily dined. As a soldier will say farewell to his little children first and then draw apart for a final farewell with that one who understands and loves him most, his wife, so Christ separated himself from his family of apostles and called to him the three who loved and understood Him best of all: Peter, James and John. Then it was that "he began to be sorrowful, and sore troubled. Then saith he unto them, My soul is exceeding sorrowful, even unto death: abide ye here, and watch with me." (Matt. 26:37 f., ASV)

II. *The Cause of His Agony*

What was the cause of this amazement, sorrow, and great trouble even unto death which our Lord endured in Gethsemane? It was a taste of the cup He was about to drink. He always knew that He was to die; He had predicted it many times; He had set His face as flint to go to Jerusalem where He was to be delivered up. He had discussed with Moses and Elijah His decease at Jerusalem. It was not a disclosure that He was to drink a cup of woe that so amazed and burdened Him that He sweat great drops of blood. It must have been a divinely given realization of what that cup of suffering was—not just that it was to be, but *what* it was to be. He had always known that He was to die and be separated from God on the cross; now He was made to feel what it was. In the words of Jonathan Edwards: "The sorrow and distress which his soul then suffered, arose from that lively, and full, and immediate view which he had then given him of that cup of wrath; by which God the Father did as it were set the cup down before him, for him to take it and drink it. Some have inquired, what was the occasion of that distress and agony, and many speculations there have been about it, but the account which the Scripture itself gives us is sufficiently full in this matter and does not leave room for speculation or doubt. The thing that Christ's mind was so full of at that time was, without doubt, the same as that which his mouth was so full of: it was the dread which his feeble nature had of that dreadful cup, which was vastly more terrible than Nebuchadnezzar's fiery furnace. He had then a near view of that furnace of wrath, into which he was to be cast; he was brought to the mouth of the furnace that he might look into it, and stand and view its raging flames, and see the glowings of its heat, that he might know where he was going and what he was about to suffer. This was the thing that filled his soul with sorrow and darkness, this terrible sight as it were overwhelmed him. For what was that human nature of Christ to such mighty wrath as this? It was in itself, without the supports of God, but a feeble worm of the dust, a thing that was crushed before the moth. None of God's children ever had such a cup set before them, as this first being of every creature had."

The second Adam was undergoing a much greater temptation than the first one. The probation was the same, however, testing obedience to God. There is, however, no indication that Adam faced anything comparable to the ordeal of Christ in His obedience. Adam was to obey God by not eating of the tree. We may assume that there was something very tempting— even without the solicitation of Satan—in that tree's fruit. But certainly that trial could not approach the ordeal of Christ. He had to be obedient unto death; Adam had to be obedient unto life. Adam's obedience would save him from death; Christ's obedience would deliver Him to death. Furthermore, Christ could see in advance all the horror of that death which obedience would cost. Never had there been or could there be a temptation like that.

The preview of impending doom was so terrifying that the mighty Jesus Himself asked, if it were possible, to escape it. Normally His obedience was in-

stant and without question. Only the extreme severity
of the ordeal can explain the plea: "O my Father, if
it be possible, let this cup pass from me." The Son
appealed directly to His loving Father to save Him
from this hour if it were by any means possible. Mark
tells us that He even first reminded God of His ability
to do all things as He said: "Abba [a term of utmost
filial intimacy], Father, all things are possible unto
thee; . . ." To the same effect, Luke mentions that
He said: "Father, if thou be willing, . . ." In John, on
an occasion which appears to be identical with the
one we are considering, Jesus said, "Father, save me
from this hour." The fact that this appeal appears in
all accounts and the poignancy with which it is recorded show clearly how fervently Christ must have
asked about the possibility of escaping the dread hour.

It is not said that God answered His Son's plea on
this occasion. There were other occasions when God
did speak audibly from Heaven so that His Son and
those about could hear Him. On this occasion God
seems to have been silent, but the Son knew the
answer. Indeed, I think it was a rhetorical question—
a question to which the answer was already known. It
was a cry of desperation, and not an inquiry at all.
Jesus knew that if there had been any conceivable
way whereby God could have redeemed the world
other than by the horrible death of His Son, God
would never have resorted to such an expedient. He
knew that there never could be any other name given

under Heaven whereby men must be saved. He knew there was none other good enough to pay the price of sin; none other could open the door and let us in. Jesus knew that if those dear ones whom He had left were to drink of the vine again with Him in the kingdom of God, there was but one way—He must drink of the cup of God's wrath.

III. Christ's Self-Surrender to Agony

So, looking directly into the furnace of the coming divine fury into which His own willing obedience alone could cause Him to be cast, Christ said: "Nevertheless not as I will, but as thou wilt." He made God's will His will, even though He knew fully and terribly what such submission meant. God's will was His will. The Father and the Son were one in their redemptive love for the elect. This is made even more explicit in John's account, where Christ says: "Father, save me from this hour: but for this cause came I unto this hour Father, glorify thy name."

"And he cometh unto the disciples, and findeth them asleep, and saith unto Peter, What, could ye not watch with me one hour?" The Saviour was surrendering Himself to the wrath of God for His people. He had asked His chief disciples just to stand by—to understand and to appreciate and to comfort. He did not ask them to do anything else. There was nothing they could do. It was because they could do *nothing* that Christ had to do *everything* for their redemption.

But could they not even stand by? Could they not sorrow that He had to suffer so for them? Could they not even stay awake for one hour? What a heart-breaking ordeal to find those for whom He was about to die unable to stay awake for an hour to comfort Him in His great and terrible vicarious death for them! Yet our Lord, overwhelmed with the vision He has just had of the fiery torment before Him, to which He would submit Himself for the elect's sake, very gently chides His sleeping disciples. Immediately He turns from His own concerns to their needs. "Love seeketh not her own," and so Love Incarnate quickly forgets His anguish and turns to the disciples' needs. Affectionately He warns them, not for His sake but for their own, "Watch and pray, that ye enter not into temptation: the spirit indeed is willing, but the flesh is weak." In that remark, grief-stricken as He was, bitterly disappointed as He must have been, Christ does not fail to notice and even praise the drowsy disciples for having the right spirit and meaning well, even though they were so very weak.

IV. Christ's Source of Strength in Agony

Then the Saviour departs from the apostles a second time and prays again. "O my Father, if this cup may not pass away from me, except I drink it, thy will be done." The agony of the first prayer is not over, but a new note is detectable. Realizing that it was not possible for the cup to pass from Him, and still agonizing at the thought of its horror, our Lord is now more definitely praying for the strength to drink the cup of God's wrath. As man He had shrunk from the cup; as man He will drink it; as man He looks to the Father for strength. In John's account He prays: "Father, glorify thy name." Luke tells us that an angel came and ministered unto Him. Having submitted Himself to His sacrifice, He knows that He needs great strength to endure the cross. As a man, He was not equal to it. He looks to his heavenly Father, who has willed His death, to enable Him to perform what has become His own will also. John tells us that on this occasion God does speak, saying: "I both have glorified it, and will glorify it." Possibly in connection with that promise, God sent an angel to minister to His Son.

The Redeemer was following the same pattern of prayer which He had taught to His disciples. First He had asked that God's will be done. Then He asked for his daily bread, that is, His strength for the day. God's will was difficult to perform, and only God could enable even the Son of man Himself to perform it. "Command what thou wilt, and give what thou commandest." That He needed superhuman strength desperately is shown in His asking God for the third time to do His will through Him. All the while the apostles, who needed strength so much more than the mighty Son, instead of maintaining their vigil during His, slept. In the sequel, the One who watched and prayed walked quietly to His horrible death while those who slept were scattered by mere danger.

When Christ gave His cheek to the betrayer's kiss, He knew that He was putting the cup of wrath to His lips, the full dregs of which He would not taste until the morrow when He would cry out, "*Eloi, Eloi, lama sabachthani?* . . . My God, my God, why hast thou forsaken me?"

V. Those For Whom Christ Endured His Agony

This, then, is how Jesus made atonement—how He paid it all. The punishment which was due to us He voluntarily received. The death which was the wages of our sin He underwent. The stripes with which we deserved to be beaten fell upon His willing back. The chastisement which was owing us was borne by Him. The price we would have paid by endless suffering He paid by an infinite sacrifice. It should have been I who cried out, "My God, my God, why hast thou forsaken me?" It should have been He who said: "I am persuaded that nothing shall separate me from the love of God." Because Jesus paid it all, it was He who was forsaken and we who never shall be. Because He drank the full cup of divine wrath, we shall never taste it. "There is therefore now no condemnation to them that are in Christ Jesus."

CHAPTER VI

Justification by Faith: Twofold Salvation

FROM CHAPTER 1:18 to 3:20 of the Epistle to the Romans, the Apostle Paul seeks to demonstrate the universal sinfulness of men. He shows the wrath of God revealed against the heathen because they would not have God in their thinking. He shows that the nominally religious people of Israel, by their condemning other persons for sins of which they were also guilty, were treasuring up "wrath against the day of wrath." In the third chapter Paul shows that all have gone astray. "There is none that doeth good." With the law or without the law, men have sinned. Every mouth is stopped. The whole world is shut up under judgment. Then and then only does the Apostle come back to his theme, saying: "Now the righteousness of God without [apart from] the law is manifested [revealed], being witnessed by the law and the prophets; even the righteousness of God which is by faith of Jesus Christ unto all and upon all them that believe: for there is no difference: for all have sinned, and come short of the glory of God; being justified freely by his grace through the redemption that is in Christ Jesus: whom God hath set forth to be a propitiation through faith in his blood, to declare his righteousness for the remission of sins that are past, through the forbearance of God; to declare, I say, at this time his righteousness: that he might be just, and the justifier of him which believeth in Jesus" (Rom. 3:21-26).

Having shown most plainly that no man can be saved by the works of the law, Paul proceeds to show, just as plainly, that men may be saved by the faith that is in Christ Jesus. Now that he has shown men why they should not trust in themselves, he will show them how suitable it is to trust in Christ. Since their own works only condemn them, he will tell them of One whose works can save them. Futhermore, he says that this is no novel way of salvation. It is the only way of salvation in all ages. Abraham was saved this way, and so was David. In the beginning of chapter four Paul points out that "if Abraham were justified by works, he hath whereof to glory; but not before God. For what saith the scripture? Abraham believed God, and it was counted unto him for righteousness." In verse 5 he gives us a classic statement of justification by faith alone. "To him that worketh not, but believeth on him that justifieth the ungodly, his faith is counted for righteouness." Justification is by faith alone without works.

I. What Justification Is

The Westminster Shorter Catechism has well summarized the abundance of biblical data on this great

theme: "Justification is an act of God's grace wherein
he pardoneth all our sins and accepteth us as righteous in his sight only for the righteousness of Christ
imputed to us and received by faith alone." Justification has a positive and a negative element. It consists
at once in the removal of guilt and the imputation, or
granting, of righteousness. It rescues the sinner as a
brand from the burning and at the same time gives
him a title to Heaven. If it failed to do either of
these, it would fail to do anything. For man, as a
sinner against God, must have that enormous guilt
somehow removed. But, at the same time, if he had
the guilt removed, he would still be devoid of positive
righteousness and with no title to Heaven and would
also be certain to fall again into sin and condemnation. If Christ only cancelled out guilt, He would
merely return the sinner to Adam's original state
without Adam's original perfection of nature. There
must be the "double cure."

> Rock of Ages, cleft for me,
> Let me hide myself in Thee;
> Let the water and the blood,
> From Thy riven side which flowed,
> Be of sin the double cure,
> Cleanse me from its guilt and power.

This epistle has already shown us that men are
guilty before God. Their sins have incurred the
wrath of God ("the wrath of God is revealed from
heaven against all ungodliness and unrighteousness

of men, who hold the truth in unrighteousness"
—Rom. 1:18), and this wrath is further intensified by
every sin that is committed (by your hard and "impenitent heart treasurest up wrath against the day of
wrath and the revelation of the righteous judgment of
God"—Rom. 2:5). Later, the same epistle tells us
that the "wages of sin is death" (Rom. 6:23). Death
refers to eternal death in Hell because it is set in contrast with eternal life. Had Christ Himself not said
the same thing? "The Son of man came not to be
ministered unto, but to minister, and to give his life
a ransom for many" (Matt. 20:28). "This," He said,
"is my body which is given for you" (Luke 22:19).
Had He not said that like "as Moses lifted up the
serpent in the wilderness, even so must the Son of
man be lifted up" (John 3:14)? Why should the
Son of man be lifted up as a vile serpent, the symbol
of sin, to become sin, and cry out in His desolation,
"My God, my God, why hast thou forsaken me?"
(Matt. 27:46) except that, as Paul says, God made
Him who knew no sin to become sin for us "that we
might become the righteousness of God in him"
(II Cor. 5:21, ASV). Christ Himself did not say so
much about His death. He was making the sacrifice;
He left to others the privilege of explaining it. For
two thousand years now the church has been glorying
in His cross and exploring its wondrous meaning.

The positive element, the making just or righteous,
is really the central aspect of justification, though it is

commonly less noticed. But, as we have said, if Christ did not procure our righteousness as well as secure our remission, the latter would have been of no avail to us, for we would still be outside Paradise and exposed to the recurrence of sin and ultimate damnation. God could not bestow righteousness on us, to be sure, without removing our filthy guilt. But, on the other hand, it would have been no use to remove our guilt if He did not bestow a new righteousness on us. This is what the first Adam failed to do. He was never asked to die for the remission of sin, but he was placed on probation to fulfill the law and secure the perpetual favor of God upon all whom he represented. He failed in this. The second Adam, the man Christ Jesus, both washed us from our sins by His blood and clothed us in the white raiment of His righteousness, justified.

In order to do this great thing, Christ had first to be justified Himself so that in His justification those whom He represented might share. This He did. He fulfilled the law perfectly, not for Himself alone but for His people. He was holy and undefiled—a lamb without blemish. He was one who could say, "The prince of this world cometh, and hath nothing in me." He was the Son in whom the Father was well pleased, made in all points like as we are, but without sin. Therefore God vindicated the second Adam, as we read in I Peter 3:18: "For Christ also hath once suffered for sins, the just for the unjust, that he might bring us to God, being put to death in the flesh but quickened by the Spirit." In I Timothy 3:16: "Without controversy great is the mystery of godliness: God was manifest in the flesh, justified in the Spirit, seen of angels, preached unto the Gentiles, believed on in the world, received up into glory." Here it is seen that the man Christ Jesus was justified by His own keeping of the law, but in Romans 4:25 we see that this justification was not for Himself alone but representatively for His people: "Who was delivered up for our offences, and was raised again for our justification. " So I Timothy tells us that He was raised again for His own justification and Romans 4:25 that He was raised again for our justification. In justification, as in all other works of the Mediator, He does not act as a private person, but as a public one; not for Himself alone, but for all of His own; not for the Head only but for the members of the body as well. So that we are quickened, raised up, and made to sit together in heavenly places in Christ Jesus. You are Christ's, and Christ is God's. Again in Romans 8:34: "Who is he that condemneth? It is Christ that died, yea rather, that is risen again, who is even at the right hand of God, who also maketh intercession for us." So, being justified, being endowed with a title to life as well as a reprieve from death, "we have peace with God, . . . access into this grace wherein we stand, and rejoice [triumphantly] in hope of the glory of God."

That these two elements together constitute justification is shown in Acts 26:18: "that they may receive forgiveness of sins, and inheritance among them which are sanctified by faith that is in me." Also John 5:24: "He that heareth my word, and believeth on him that sent me, hath everlasting life, and shall not come into condemnation."

II. *That Justification Is by Faith in Christ*

Why is faith the means of justification? Is it a kind of good work? No, for the Bible is very plain in teaching that salvation is not by works of any kind. If it were, we would have whereof to glory. We could not boast that we did this or that or the other thing, but we could glory in our belief. "Nothing in my hands I bring," we could sing, "except my faith." No other work could avail, only the work of believing. If faith were a kind of good work, we would be back again at the old heresy of salvation by works; but now it would be the work of faith. Romans 4:5 makes it clear that we are not saved by faith as a good work. For that text says that we are justified while still ungodly in ourselves. God "justifieth the ungodly." So, at the moment of justification we are still ungodly. If we are still ungodly then, our faith cannot be a good work.

But why is faith the means of justification? Simply because it is the action of union with Jesus Christ. Faith is our coming to Him, our trusting Him, our resting in Him. The moment we are united to Him, we are immediately endowed with all that He has secured for us. We are immediately justified before we have done a single good deed, because we are His and He is God's. Just as a very poor woman is a very poor woman until the very moment that she marries a wealthy man. But at the moment that she becomes his wife, she becomes a wealthy woman. It is by means of her acceptance that she becomes a wealthy woman, but her acceptance does not make her a wealthy woman; it is her husband's wealth that makes her so. So faith does not justify; Christ justifies. But faith is the act of union with Christ.

A. H. Strong uses the analogy of the coupling. The coupling joins a train of cars to a locomotive. The coupling has no power in itself. It cannot move a single car an inch. All the power is in the locomotive. But the coupling is the link by which the power of the locomotive is transmitted to the cars. Faith has no power in itself; it is not a ground of salvation; it is not a good work. It is merely that by which all the goodness and grace and glory of Christ comes to the sinner.

III. Justification Is by Faith Without Works

How emphatically Romans 4:5 states this central truth of the Bible! "But to him THAT WORKETH NOT, but BELIEVETH on him that justifieth the UNGODLY, his FAITH is COUNTED for righteousness." From this verse we learn that: (a) the justified person is one that worketh not; (b) he believes rather than does; (c) he is ungodly when justified rather than godly or one who has something to his credit; (d) it is his faith, not his deeds, that is the instrument of his justification; and (e) his justification is counted or reckoned to him rather than awarded him on the basis of merit. If it were possible to state the gratuitousness of justification more clearly than this, we doubt if even divine inspiration could find the words. Five separate expressions in one part of a sentence setting forth the absolute freeness of salvation leave no room to doubt that the way to God is wide open. There is nothing standing between the sinner and his God. He has immediate and unimpeded access to the Savior. There is nothing to hinder. No sin can hold him back, because God offers justification to the ungodly. Nothing now stands between the sinner and God but the sinner's "good works." Nothing can keep him from Christ but his delusion that he does not need Him—that he has good works of his own that can satisfy God. If men will only be convinced that they have no righteousness that is not as filthy rags; if men will see that there is none that doeth good, no, not one; if men will see that all are shut up under sin—then there will be nothing to prevent their everlasting salvation. All they need is need. All they must have is nothing. All that is required is acknowledged guilt. Only confess your sins. But, alas, sinners cannot part with their "virtues."

They have none that are not imaginary, but they are real to them. So grace becomes unreal. The real grace of God they spurn in order to hold on to the illusory virtues of their own. Their eyes fixed on a mirage, they will not drink real water. They die of thirst with water all about them.

Why do men not accept the gospel? How can they refuse the tender overtures of the gracious Son of God? Why do they even take offense at the cross? Let us consider an analogy. An etiquette book is a very valuable accessory. It is useful on many important occasions. A good one costs considerable money. Who would not be glad to have one, if it were given him? You wouldn't? Why wouldn't you be glad to be given such a book? Because it would imply you needed it! That is the reason proud sinners do not come to Christ. Their coming would imply they needed Him. They are too proud and self-righteous in their natural state to admit that!

CHAPTER VII

Sanctification: Christianizing the Christian

C HRISTIAN PERFECTION is an ideal for which we must all strive. Although there is a double standard of morality in Romish theology, Protestant Christianity knows no such distinction. The priesthood of all believers is a well-known Reformation principle. The perfection of all believers (as a duty) is another cardinal Protestant principle. Some professed Protestants expect their ministers to be perfect, while they think of themselves as under a less demanding ideal. Officers of the church are expected to strive for the ideal, which for the others is regarded as a mere word.

Officers cannot for a moment allow the people to get away with this double standard. Not that there is any objection to demanding perfection of ministers— God does this; but there is an objection to laymen not demanding perfection of themselves. Still, granting all this, there is peculiar propriety in officers applying themselves to the pursuit of perfection. The fact that all Christians are required by God to be perfect does not make that duty less but more binding on those who are to lead and correct the people in the things of God. After all, the snuffers in the ancient tabernacle were made of pure gold, as Matthew Henry observed.

"It appears singular to the reader of St. Paul's Epistles," writes W. G. T. Shedd, "that the apostle in one passage speaks of Christians as perfect, and in another as imperfect. At one time, he describes them in terms that would lead us to infer that they are holy as God is holy; and at another, he speaks of them as full of sin and corruption. In the text, he denominates them 'the elect of God, holy and beloved,' and yet immediately proceeds to exhort them to the possession and practice of the most common Christian graces— such as humility and forgiveness. In a preceding paragraph, he tells the Colossians that they 'are dead to sin, and their life is hid with Christ in God,' and then goes on to urge them to overcome some of the most gross sins in the whole catalogue—'mortify, therefore, your members which are upon the earth; fornication, uncleanness, inordinate affection, evil concupiscence, and covetousness, which is idolatry' (Col. 3:3-5) ."

The Bible teaches these three things concerning perfection: first, that the Christian in one sense is perfect; second, that in another sense, he needs to become perfect; and, third, what he is to do about it. These points will determine our treatment of the theme of Christian santification.

1. The Sense in Which the Christian Is Already Perfect

The Bible clearly states that there is a sense in which the Christian is already holy. Colossians 3:12, for example, states: "Put on therefore, as the elect of God, holy and beloved, bowels of mercies, kindness, humbleness of mind, meekness, longsuffering."

Christians are already holy and perfect in two respects: first, they are actually justified or declared righteous; second, they are sanctified (set apart as holy) in principle, or potentially righteous. This first form of holiness is that which is imputed or reckoned to us; namely, the holiness of Christ which becomes ours through faith. He who knew no sin became sin that we might become the righteousness of God in Him. Christ took the guilt of our sin, and we received the merit of His righteousness. We are now clothed in the white garments of the spotless lamb of God that took away the sin of the world. This is the righteousness we received when first we believed. "Justification is an act of God's free grace, wherein he pardoneth all our sins and accepteth us as righteous in his sight, only for the righteousness of Christ imputed unto us, and received by faith alone." So then in this sense, a person is holy, perfectly holy, from the moment he first becomes a Christian.

We are already holy in a second respect; that is, we are sanctified in principle. We have a new living principle within which is certainly destined to conquer our old and sinful nature. It is so certain that this new principle is dominant and shall win out over the evil principle which is mortally wounded at conversion that we Christians are spoken of at times as if we already had won the victory and were already perfectly holy. This is a common way of speaking. For example, on Friday I reached a certain stage in the preparation of a paper on which I was working. I knew that it was then as good as finished. I considered my work virtually completed. The outcome was a practical certainty. To be sure, there was a good deal more work to do, more research to complete, and so on; but fundamentally the back of the job was broken. So I was able to mow the lawn with peace of mind. As J. W. A. Stewart put it: "When the 21st of March has come we say the back of winter is broken. There will still be alternations of frost, but the progress will be towards heat. The coming of summer is sure; in germ the summer is already here."

So the believer is holy in the sense that that which is in him is mightier than that which is in the world. The ultimate triumph of this principle of life in Christ Jesus is certain. The saint is as good as sanctified. His seed abideth (I John 3:9). This is present holiness, which every Christian now possesses and without which no man shall see the Lord.

The holiness of imputed righteousness and principial sanctification are illustrated in the following

simile: " 'The steamship whose machinery is broken
may be brought into port and made fast to the dock.
She is *safe*, but not *sound*. Repairs may last a long
time. Christ designs to make us both safe and sound.
Justification gives the first—safety; sanctification gives
the second—soundness.' " (quoted by A. H. Strong in
Systematic Theology, p. 869)

II. *The Sense in Which the Christian Is Now Imperfect*

The saint's imperfection is no less apparent than
his perfection. It jumps right out from the Scripture.
In Colossians 3:12 we are told that Christians are elect
and holy; immediately after, we are exhorted to put
on mercy, humility, and the other elements of a holy
life. In the Lord's Prayer we are specifically instructed to ask God for the forgiveness of our debts, or
sins. Paul counted himself not to have attained; he
did not consider himself already perfect. The Apostle
John, one of the most saintly men of all time, the beloved of the Lord, said that if any man said he had
no sin he deceived himself and the truth was not in
him. A preacher, commenting on the fact that the
Christian who says he has no sin deceives himself,
remarked that he does not deceive anyone but himself. Luther likened the sanctification of the Christian to the healing of an open sore. The sore is healing, is potentially healed; but meanwhile it is quite
painful and may be putrid.

III. *What the Christian Is to Do in This Situation*

In this situation the Christian is called upon to strive for the very perfection which he already potentially enjoys. That is what a great artist does when he trains to become a great artist. We know that Enrico Caruso and Fritz Kreisler had music in their souls at the beginning. Training for them meant making their potential genius actual. If it had not been there to begin with, no amount of training would have produced it. But, even though it were there, it would never have come to expression and reality without training. So the Christian has the gift of religious genius. It is given to him at his birth as a Christian (regeneration). He is then called upon to bring it out; the process is called Christian education (from *educare*, to lead out). In the Colossians passage, Paul says, "put on," or "put forth." "Put on therefore, as the elect of God, holy and beloved, bowels of mercies, kindness, humbleness of mind, meekness, longsuffering." That is, "You are holy; therefore put forth these holy acts of mercy, humility, meekness, and longsuffering."

"You" put on or put forth these virtues. "You" do this; not God. A certain modern movement calls upon its adherents to "let go and let God." But Christianity does not say, "Let go"; it says, "Put forth." The Sandemanians were an obscure little sect which taught the deadliness of all doing and the necessity for inactivity in order to let God do his work in the soul. But Christianity says, "Work out your own salvation with fear and trembling. For it is God which worketh in you."

Just how God works and we work is beautifully illustrated by the great Dutch theologian, Abraham Kuyper:

> You can represent this to yourself most vividly when you think of a ship.
>
> At the stern of that ship is a rudder, and attached to this rudder is the tiller, and this is held by the hand of the helmsman.
>
> Should there be no steering when at sea, this boat moves under the action of the wind and waves, then when the ship turns the rudder turns, when the rudder turns the tiller turns, and with it the hand and the arm of the man at the helm moves involuntarily back and forth.
>
> Behold the image of a will-less man.
>
> He is adrift upon the sea of life. As wind and waves drive, so he is driven along, under influences from without and from within—of circumstances, of his passion. And as life makes him go, now in this direction, now in that, so he goes; and so turns the rudder in his inward purpose, and so turns the tiller and the hand at the helm; *i.e.,* his will.
>
> The will-less one!
>
> But it is altogether different when there is steerage in the ship. Then the man at the helm keeps the course. He knows where he wants to go. And

when wind and wave would drive him out of his course, he works against them. Then his hand grasps the tiller firmly, he turns it, and therewith the rudder itself, against wind and wave. And the ship that responds to the helm, cuts through the waves, not as tide and wind would direct it, but as the helmsman wills.

Such is the man of character, the man with will-perception and will-power, who does not drift, but steers.

But there is still a third point.

On the bridge of the ship, far away from the helm, stands the captain, and he has placed a helmsman at the tiller. Now the captain on the bridge must know what course the ship must take. On the bridge he stands much higher, and therefore knows far better how the ship must point to the right or to the left. And so the helmsman has but this single duty, namely, that he listen to what the captain on the bridge commands, and that he carries out those orders.

Applied to the soul, God is this Captain on the bridge, and we are the man at the helm. And if, with the tiller of the small boat of our soul in hand, we but will what God wills, and so turn the helm to right or left as God commands, then no danger need be feared, and presently through wind and wave the little boat enters safely the desired haven.

If this goes on through the whole of life, we grow accustomed to it; we know at length by anticipation, whether the Captain on the bridge will command

left or right. Thus, of ourselves we come to know
God's will more and more. And this knowledge of
God brings us nearer to the haven of salvation,—to
eternal life.

When God so works in upon our self that at length
we will what God wills, the process is not external
but internal. (*To Be Near Unto God,* The Macmil-
lan Co., 1925, pp. 200-202.)

But to come back to our point. We must put on
holiness. It is not enough to know how it is done. It
must be done. It is not enough to know that it must
be done, we must *do* it. Though I have all knowledge
to understand all mysteries and have not love, it
profits me nothing. Dr. A. H. Strong in his *Systematic
Theology* quotes Dr. Hastings, who told of an occasion when the great French preacher Bourdaloue was
probing the conscience of Louis XIV, applying to him
the words of St. Paul and intending to paraphrase
them: "For the good which I would, I do not, but the
evil which I would not, that I do," "I find two men
in me"—the King interrupted the great preacher with
the memorable exclamation: "Ah, these two men, I
know them well!" Bourdaloue answered: "It is already something to *know* them, Sire; but it is not
enough,—one of the two must perish."

But, how do we actually put on these virtues which
make for Christian perfection? How do we put them
forth? How do we exhibit them so that men may see
our good works and glorify our Father who is in

Heaven? Two things are called for: meditation and exercise.

By meditation we practice the presence of Christ. If we would run with patience the race that is set before us, we must look to Jesus, the author and finisher of our faith. And if we would look to Jesus we will search His Word (John 5:39). We are transformed by the renewing of our minds; by letting the mind be in us which was in Christ Jesus. We know how association with great and good persons has a profound effect upon us. Gamaliel Bradford, the celebrated biographer, said that he "lived" with Robert E. Lee for many years and it made him a better man. He "lived" with Mark Twain for years and it made him a worse man. When Saint-Gaudens was given the job of making a statue of Phillips Brooks, he studied the man carefully. The famous sculptor came to realize that in order to understand Brooks he had to understand Brooks' Christ. So he read the Gospels, lived with Christ, and at last he gave his life to Christ. Chalmers spoke of the expulsive power of a new affection; it also has a propulsive power. "The love of Christ constraineth us; because we thus judge that if one died for all, then were all dead: and that he died for all that they which live should not henceforth live unto themselves, but unto him which died for them, and rose again" (II Cor. 5:14-15). So let us practice the presence of God.

And then exercise! How do we put on virtues?

"By taking every occasion to exercise them . . . Strain day after day upon a particular muscle, and it will begin to swell and rise above the flesh. You do not create the muscle by this effort, but you stimulate and strengthen it . . . There is too much Christian character lying dormant and latent, because there is so much neglect of self-culture in the Church." Church officers and other leaders have a big job. We never hold a retreat in our church without some officer learning, as it were, for the first time how really big his job is, and wanting to resign forthwith. If that happened, there would be literal retreats. But that is not the purpose of a "retreat"; it is, rather, merely drawing back to see the job whole so that we may advance to it. You have the gift for your respective ministries—just exercise it, and you will know you have it.

The same applies to all Christians. Develop some spiritual muscle. You who are holy, grow in holiness; you who are perfect, be ye perfect as your Father in Heaven is perfect. Philippians 3:13-14: "Brethren, I count not myself to have apprehended: but this one thing I do, forgetting those things which are behind, and reaching forth unto those things which are before, I press toward the mark for the prize of the high calling of God in Christ Jesus." If the Apostle Paul needed spiritual exercise, do you, my dear reader, not need it?

CHAPTER VIII

Assurance: How We Know That We Know Christ

UP TO THIS POINT our interest has been in coming to Christ. We have considered our lost condition by nature, our need of a Saviour, and Christ's remarkable qualifications for that role, and the way by which we are persuaded of it. But now we address ourselves to the question of how we know that we have truly come to Christ, or how we know that we truly know Christ. Conceivably a person could come to Christ without being certain that he is actually united to him. Presumably, a person could think that he had come to Christ without really doing so. And presumably a person could truly come to Christ and know it. Now what we here want to discover is how we know that we know Christ.

In previous chapters we have thought about our sinfulness and how we came to be sinful, and about Christ, His deity and His mediatorial work. All of these were doctrines which could be ascertained objectively and were in a sense external to us. Now we are dealing with something which we can only know by our self-examination. We are to search into our own souls to see if we have a certain experience. At the same time we are being objective, in this sense: we are studying the Word of God to ascertain the evidences for which we must search. While we are considering what the evidences of a saved condition are, we will be asking ourselves whether we possess these qualifications. At that point the discussion is both objective and subjective.

Many indications of a regenerate condition are mentioned in the Scripture. As a matter of fact, there are too many of them for us to consider in this brief chapter. We will, therefore, restrict ourselves to one passage which we will use as a guide in this discussion. We will, however, refer to other passages incidentally but not primarily.

The passage which will serve as a foundation of our discussion here is Romans 5:1-3. "Therefore being justified by faith, we have peace with God through our Lord Jesus Christ: by whom also we have access by faith into this grace wherein we stand, and rejoice in hope of the glory of God. And not only so, but we glory in tribulations also: knowing that tribulation worketh patience." In this passage the Apostle is giving us the argument from experience. In the immediately foregoing passage, the fourth chapter, he has shown the experience of the patriarchs of old, Abraham and David. Now he turns away from the past to the present and speaks of the experience of the

Roman Christians, saying, "Therefore being justified by faith, *we* have . . ."

I. First Indication of Justification: Peace

The first fruit of justification, or, we may say, the first evidence of our being in a justified state, is peace. Says the Apostle, "Therefore being justified by faith, we have peace with God through our Lord Jesus Christ."

Before we can consider the peace here mentioned, we must first of all notice a minor textual matter. The King James and the Revised Standard Version represent Paul as saying, "we have peace." However, Paul did not actually write that. He wrote, rather, "let us have peace." There is little doubt among the scholars that he did indeed actually write *echōmen* and not *echomen*. He very probably used the subjunctive and not the indicative. Why, then, do they not simply translate it "let us have" instead of rendering it "we have"? Well, most of the scholars are frank enough to say that they render it in the indicative because they believe that is the thrust of Paul's thought even though he does use a subjunctive word. That is, most interpreters feel that the argument of Romans is so logical and so relentless and so obvious that at this particular point Paul can be making nothing but a declaration. There cannot be anything tentative or uncertain, hypothetical or hortatory, about it. So, in spite of the language which the Apostle uses, the translators construe him otherwise because they feel his thought demands it. We sympathize with these translators and agree with their general appraisal of Paul's thought here. Nevertheless, we consider it a very serious matter to change an inspired author's word. We prefer, therefore, to leave the subjunctive just as the Apostle gave it to us.

What is the significance then of the fact that Paul did use the subjunctive and that he wrote: "let us have peace"? Does it somehow diminish the force of this passage because he used a subjunctive rather than an indicative? We think not. As a matter of fact, we are inclined to think that it may, if we understand properly, show a greater significance and contribute more to the movement of Paul's thought than the indicative would.

We mean this: Paul could never tell these Christians, or urge them, or exhort them, to have peace unless he believed that peace had actually been established by God through justification. His subjunctive, in other words, presupposes a prior indicative. That is, Paul is exhorting the Romans here to have peace in the sense of experiencing peace because peace already has them. That is, peace already has been established and they therefore have every right and duty to appropriate it, to enjoy it, to revel in it. So I rather suspect that the Apostle is far ahead of his translators here. The translators are holding back at the indicative which Paul has already assumed and moved beyond. The point, however, as far as we here are concerned is that the subjunctive necessarily implies the indicative. The exhortation to have peace presupposes that peace has already been established. That is, a man could never be urged by Paul to experience a peace which the Apostle did not believe was already effected between that man and God. We remember that in Romans 1:18 Paul had already said that "the wrath of God is revealed from heaven against all ungodliness and unrighteousness of men, . . ." Now if the wrath of God were still burning against mankind the Apostle would certainly never urge men to have peace. Nowhere in these early chapters where he is shutting up all under divine judgment and exposing them to the wrath of God does he, or could he, urge them to have peace. It is only after the grace of God in Christ and justification by faith is introduced that Paul urges his readers to have peace with God.

Coming now to the peace of God itself, we notice the first great fruit or mark of justification here mentioned. This is indication that there is no longer any estrangement between the holy God and the former sinner who was under His wrath and judgment. If a person has peace established and is in a position to experience, feel, and rejoice in this peace, this is a true indication that he has actually a genuine union with Jesus Christ.

This, however, immediately raises a question. Is it possible that a person could wrongly think that he was justified and therefore think that he had peace established between God and him and then actually feel in his heart this peace to which the Apostle exhorts him? In other words, while a truly justified person will have this fruit of justification, namely peace, is it still not possible for people who only *think* they have justification to feel a peace which flows from it, which peace is spurious and quite misleading? Is experienced peace a true indication of a person's converted state? Putting it in the form of a question, Can we know that we know Christ because we have the experience of peace? Obviously, if it is possible to have a spurious feeling of peace, the feeling can be no sure indication that a person has justification or has Jesus Christ.

Yes, it is possible to distinguish between true and spurious peace. Peace may be a feeling, but it rests on some presumed fact which may be logically grasped and evaluated. If you ask some persons why they feel at peace with God, they will answer, "Because God never hates or becomes truly angry with anyone." They suppose that God need never be feared. So they have a variety of peace. The doctrine on which it rests is unscriptural and therefore false and *ipso facto*; it is spurious. If, however, a person feels peace and knows that it results from faith that Christ satisfied divine justice for him and converted his soul and united him to the Saviour, the peace he feels is genuine since it rests on the truth of God.

II. Second Indication of Justification: Fellowship

The second proof of one's salvation that the Apostle mentions is a gracious state. "We have access by faith into this grace wherein we stand." The grace here mentioned signifies a condition of fellowship with God. It introduces us to a second level of Christian experience. It is a distinct advance upon the previously mentioned peace which we have and may experience with God. There could have been peace established without any subsequent fellowship. Peace itself signifies merely the cessation of hostilities. It does not necessarily mean the resumption, or the introduction, of friendship. It could be an armed truce or a state of belligerency or a cold war. Peace simply means the absence of hostilities, expressed hostility. Of course, the peace of God is more than merely an armed truce. It does signify that there is no remaining hostility, outward or inward, hot or cold. Nevertheless, the word "peace" itself does not signify anything more than precisely that. Peace can be established without a condition of intimacy and love and fellowship obtaining. But this word "grace" signifies precisely that a condition of fellowship and love does obtain after the peace has been established.

This grace which follows the peace of God could only follow peace. That is, there is no possibility of anyone having a cordial relation of friendship and love with the living God until peace is first established between them. So long as the war was on between the soul and Heaven, the soul could not suppose that God was his friend and was pleased with him. So long as the soul was at enmity with God, there could be nothing but a sense of apprehension, fear, shame, and fleeing rather than boldness, rejoicing, and loving communion. As we said, peace could be established without communion necessarily following. But now we are noticing the other side of the coin; namely, that there could be no communion without this peace.

Indeed, a part of this blessedness of fellowship with God consists in the realization of the peace which has been established. Just as truly as fear of God's wrath and judgment destroys any tranquillity between the soul and God, so the overcoming of that wrath of God suffuses the soul with a very great joy. Not only does the soul experience a vast relief, which follows the knowledge that God is no longer angry, but a positive joy as well in this wonderful knowledge.

Perhaps the most blessed characteristic of this Christian experience of fellowship with God is its inalienability. It cannot be lost. Paul indicates this by saying it is the grace "in which we stand." His word translated "stand" signifies "stand rooted," "immovable." So this fellowship, exquisite as it is in itself, is also of permanent duration.

All other joys with which we ever have any acquaintance in this life are what we may call "furlough" pleasures. As a pastor, during the last war,

I often visited families which had been torn apart by the demands of the military forces. Sometimes I visited these families when the loved husband or son or brother was home on a furlough. What a joyous occasion it was to have the family circle completed again, if only for a few days. But I doubt if I ever visited on occasions like that without seeing a mother or a wife in tears. Why? Because she usually would be anticipating that in three days or a week the loved one would be gone again. Even when she was enjoying the company of her husband or her son the joy was spoiled, to a degree, by the realization that it was soon coming to an end. Is this not true of all earthly pleasures? Are they not properly called "furlough" pleasures? They all have a terminal date. Sooner or later they will come to an end. The awareness of this fleetingness of the most exquisite of our pleasures diminishes the pleasure itself very greatly. The anticipation of the termination spoils the present enjoyment. Perhaps, in an ultimate sense, we are incapable of complete happiness unless we are relieved of the apprehension that the present phase of that happiness will be lost or diminished.

On the other hand, how wonderfully the knowledge that these pleasures will continue contributes to the present enjoyment of them. Just as truly as the realization that a present pleasure is coming to an end tends to spoil the pleasure even now, so the realization that a present pleasure is never coming to an end tends to augment the pleasure even now. When I realize that some joy will never come to an end, that realization in itself is a joy and accentuates the original joy, just as thinking that a present joy will come to an end is a disturbance and that disturbance detracts from the present joy itself.

Christian joy, fellowship in the Holy Ghost, is the only kind of pleasure, with which we are familiar in this world, which is pure, unalloyed, and augmented pleasure, because it is a grace in which we stand rooted, immovable. This is what our Lord had in mind when He said that He came that you may have life and have it abundantly. This is what the Apostle was speaking of when he called Christians conquerors and more than conquerors through Christ Jesus. This is the blessedness of those who have and to whom it shall be given which contrasts so sharply with the misery of those who have not and from whom shall be taken even that which they have.

III. Third Indication of Justification: Hope

The third fruit of justification which the Apostle mentions here is rejoicing in the hope of the glory of God. The preceding joy of fellowship with God was augmented, as we have said, by its promise. In a certain sense, that present joyful fellowship was partly from anticipation of its continuance. This matter of the future of Christian experience comes into focus when the Apostle says, "We . . . rejoice in hope of the glory of God." Here he is taking a full view of the future and telling us that the true Christian rejoices in the anticipation of it. Indeed the word "rejoices" is not quite what Paul actually said. His term would be more adequately translated as "rejoiced triumphantly." This is not only a note of happiness but of exuberant happiness. There is a certain confidence as well as a delightful anticipation. These are more than great expectations; these are great certainties for the Christian. After all, Jesus Christ gave himself that we may have life eternal. "God so loved the world, that he gave his only begotten Son, that whosoever believeth in him should not perish, but have everlasting life." That is the point of emphasis in the gospel. Not this world but the other world is the center of interest in the message of the evangel. Secularism has so permeated Christian thinking in our time that it has foreshortened the gospel picture. Even many Christians are more absorbed in this world than the other. However, Christianity and true Christian experience live under the aspect of eternity, and the Bible ends with these words, "Even so, come, Lord Jesus." The Lord's return is ever "our blessed hope" (Titus 2:13).

However glorious the experience of peace may be, however unspeakable the felicity of the Holy Ghost may be, even these blessed experiences are as nothing in comparison with what lies before. The famous evangelist, Moody, used to say, "Some day you will read in the obituaries that D. L. Moody is dead. Don't

you believe a word of it. I will have just begun to
live." That is no exaggeration. As some other person
has said, "The most wonderful five minutes in a
Christian's life are the first five minutes after death."
Jonathan Edwards, in an unpublished manuscript,
said something like this: The blessedness of Heaven
is so glorious that when the saints arrive there they
will look back upon their earthly pilgrimage, however
wonderful their life in Christ was then, as a veritable
Hell. Just as truly, on the other hand, will those
who perish in Hell look back on the life in this world,
however miserable it may have been, as veritable
Heaven [the Christian answer to those who think
that Hell is here and now].

How do we know that we know Christ? If we have
the above experiences growing out of a sound evan-
gelical belief in the gospel, we know Christ and we
know that we know Christ.

CHAPTER IX

The Church: Body of Christ

THERE ARE FUNDAMENTALLY two views of the church. There are variations of these and mixtures of them, but fundamentally only two views. This division runs through the various demoninations or "churches" as we shall see.

I. The Church Defined as Visible

The first conception of the church may be stated as follows: It is that body of persons who (1) profess faith in Christ, (2) are subordinate to properly appointed officers, and (3) associate with those of like profession and practice. We must consider these items separately.

First, they profess faith in Christ. This usually signifies more than saying they believe in someone whom they themselves call Christ. Their profession must recognize that Christ is a particular historic person who was none other than God incarnate. This is invariably considered as the minimum profession of Christianity. Insistence is on the fact that the Christ is no mere man—no mere reformer—but the very Son of God. Profession of faith in Christ may be all that is required, but this must be an orthodox profession. Usually Christ, being regarded as divine, is also recognized as a member of the Trinity. Furthermore, His divinity is seen as necessary to His work of redemption, the acknowledgement of which is usually regarded as essential. The person affirms faith in Christ—as God and Saviour.

Second, those who make this profession do so to certain men called church officers, who are thought to be appointed by Christ. After all, there must be someone, it is argued, to determine when men make satisfactory confessions. It is thought that these officers are indicated in the Bible. The Roman Catholic church finds the pope to be the recipient of the keys of the kingdom or church, and he indirectly appoints the necessary subordinates, or the priesthood. The Anglican church acknowledges no order, except administrative, higher than the bishop, who is thought to be in succession from Peter, to whom the keys were given and by whom they were transmitted to the bishopric. Those who defend the view under consideration are advocates of episcopal order, or government by bishops. Others, such as Presbyterians, believe that the officers are ministers (on one level and equal) associated with representatives of the congregation (elders) ; and still others, such as Congregationalists, regard the congregation itself as retaining and not delegating its authority.

Third, persons who profess faith in Christ to these

duly appointed officers are received into the fellowship of like-minded persons. This fellowship con-
stitutes the church. If a person professed Christ and
acknowledged certain officers but was not recognized
by them, he would not be admitted to this fellowship
and therefore would not, in spite of all, be in the
church. It is to be understood, furthermore, that
membership in this society is not inalienable. A person may be excommunicated, that is, he may be cut
off from the communion of the church and no longer
be considered a member.

This is a very understandable and apparently sound
view of the church. But is it true? Is a person who
professes faith in Christ and is received by officers
into a fellowship of like professors truly a member of
the church in the biblical sense of the word? We admit that he *may* be, but this does not satisfy advocates
of this doctrine who teach that there is no "maybe"
here but only certainty. Such a person, they say, is
undoubtedly a member of the church of Christ with
all its benefits and privileges. They will say that if a
person is a member of a certain local church or de-
nomination he is truly a member of the church of
Christ. So long as he is not cut off from the communion of this body (excommunicated) he is not
cut off from Christ. So these advocates cannot accept
our statement that members of their church *may be*
members of the church of Christ. No, say they, they
are members of Christ's church.

This notion that members of some particular de-
nomination are necessarily members of Christ's church
or body we cannot grant. We will not deny that a
person who sincerely and truly makes a sound profession of faith in Christ is a member of His true church,
but how do we (or they) know that all who make
the profession sincerely believe it? How can they be
sure that they are not receiving hypocrites? So long
as officers cannot search the hearts of professing believers, they cannot know whether such professors are
sincere, true believers or not; nor can they prevent
the admittance of some nominal (in name only) believers.

Advocates of this view must assume the officers'
ability to know the hearts of professors. But while
they assume this, they do not claim it and cannot admit that they even assume it. Even the church of
Rome claims no such infallibility for individual
priests or bishops who receive persons into their
church. So there is a dilemma here: This view de-
pends on the officers' ability to know hearts, but the
officers do not even claim such ability. Yet if they do
not have this ability, they cannot be certain that the
persons they admit are true members of the church of
Christ.

Perhaps someone will say that we are overdoing the
difficulty here. Can we not be reasonably certain that
a person who says he believes in Christ and who is
not living in any open or gross sin is a Christian? Yes,

we can be reasonably sure—that is, we can be sure enough to allow his profession to be made a basis of admission to this fellowship. But it is unreasonable to say that such a person could not possibly be a hypocrite. After all, the Bible indicates that people may say and do many things that are Christian without themselves being Christian. The rich young ruler, for example, said that he kept the whole law from his youth up, but he rejected Christ actually, even while respecting and reverencing Him. Christ said that some would come in the last day and say:"Lord, Lord, have we not prophesied in thy name? and in thy name have cast out devils? and in thy name done many wonderful works?" (Matt. 7:22). Christ did not deny their ascription of Lordship to Him, nor their claim to have prophesied, cast out devils, and done many mighty works in His name. But He rejected them nonetheless, saying: "I never knew you: depart from me, ye that work iniquity" (Matt. 7:23). The Apostle Paul wrote: "Though I speak with the tongues of men and of angels, and have not charity, I am become as sounding brass, or a tinkling cymbal. And though I have the gift of prophecy, and understand all mysteries, and all knowledge; and though I have all faith, so that I could remove mountains, and have not charity, I am nothing. And though I bestow all my goods to feed the poor, and though I give my body to be burned, and have not charity, it profiteth me nothing" (I Cor. 13:1-3). So it is possible for a person to be a great philanthropist and a martyr without having love (that is, Christ) in his heart, and all he does will therefore profit him nothing. If it is possible for a person to call Christ Lord, to cast out devils in His name and die a martyr to His cause without having Christ in his heart, then certainly no man can judge infallibly about the state of another man's soul.

It is not only that men may err in their judgments about others' profession, but they do err. Christ tells us that hypocrites are added to the professing members of His church. This is the teaching of the Parable of the Tares. An enemy plants the tares; that is, the devil establishes hypocrites in the field (or church) of Christ. Moreover, the parable could be construed as a warning to faithful church officers of their inability always to remove these "tares," or hypocrites, even when they can detect them: "lest while ye gather up the tares, ye root up also the wheat with them" (Matt. 13:29). The separation of true and false believers will not, according to this and other parables (such as the net and fishes, Matt. 13:47 f.), take place in this world but at the final judgment and not by men but by angels. Christ, though He wants us to keep His church as pure as possible, wants us to know that some inevitable impurity must be accepted and borne with until the "harvest."

II. The Church Defined as Invisible

Thus the foregoing definition of the church will

not do. The church of Christ is not simply those who profess Christ, are subordinate to his officers, and associate with those of like profession. The devil's children are members of this company. The enemies of Christ profess to love Him. This is the church of the anti-Christ as well as of Christ.

What, then, is the church of Christ? Although the foregoing definition is unsatisfactory, the addition of two words will make it quite satisfactory. Thus: The church consists of all who *sincerely* profess faith in Christ, and are *normally* subordinate to his officers and associate with those of like profession. This definition requires that the person's profession correspond to his state of heart. Since no officer can tell whether this is so, God alone knows whether the person is sincere and, therefore, truly a member of the church. For that reason the true church is called "invisible." This does not mean that true Christians are invisible but that their "trueness" or genuineness is invisible to man. For example, the true faith of the eleven apostles was not visible any more than the false faith of Judas was visible (until the betrayal and suicide following Christ's rejection of him revealed it). So long as a person makes a sound profession and does not belie it by gross sin, we "presume" that he has true faith. The Puritans used to say that we exercise a "judgment of charity." Only one thing we must avoid—namely, making a judgment of certainty.

Furthermore, we said that the church consists of all

who sincerely profess faith in Christ and are *normally* subordinate to his officers and in fellowship with those who make a like profession. Normally, sincere believers in Christ will join the "visible" church because Christ wills it. He himself attended the synagogue or church of His own day. The New Testament enjoins the assembling of ourselves together. Christ gave gifts to the church after His ascension, according to Ephesians 4:11 f., and these were ministers to build up the church. Such statements indicate that the establishment of the visible church was His will, although He forbade any to join except those who deny themselves, take up their cross, and follow Him. Hypocrites may nonetheless profess to do these things and be admitted, but that is no excuse for sincere persons not making the same profession. Christ also commanded His apostles to baptize in His name, thus receiving professors by a visible act into a visible organization. So converts to Christ desiring to do the will of Christ will receive baptism and join the visible church. At least, normally they will do all this.

Is it conceivable that they will not do this? It is not conceivable that they will permanently delay uniting with the church if they realize that it is the will of Christ that they do join. But it is conceivable, too, that they may be wrongly instructed in their duty. Hearing that they should believe and be saved, they may wrongly conclude that merely exercising and expressing faith is sufficient without joining any organization. They may not realize that belief in Christ means belief in all His commands, including the one to join the church. This is not likely, of course, and a Christian person should not long remain in such a condition. But since it is a possibility, at least in rare cases, for short intervals, we must agree with Augustine that there may be lambs outside the fold (just as there are wolves inside).

III. Biblical Use of Term "Church"

What complicates the matter is that the Bible sometimes uses the word "church" in the sense of the visible church and sometimes in the sense of the invisible church. For example, Stephen in his sermon before the Sanhedrin referred to all Israel in the wilderness as "the church." "This is he, that was in the church in the wilderness with the angel which spake to him in the mount Sina, and with our fathers: who received the lively oracles to give unto us" (Acts 7:38). Now we know that not only were there some hypocrites in that body called the "church" but almost all of the members were such. That was the generation of which God swore in his wrath that they should not enter into his rest (Ps. 95:11). Only the younger generation were spared, but the rest perished in the wilderness—a symbol of eternal perishing. Yet they were called "the church." In the apostolic church it self there were those who were not true believers, as indicated by the Apostle John in I John 2:19: "They went out from us, but they were not of us; for if they had been of us, they would no doubt have continued with us: but they went out, that they might be made manifest that they were not all of us."

On the other hand, the true church is mentioned, too. Christ said: "I will build my church; and the gates of Hell shall not prevail against it" (Matt. 16: 18). The powers of Hell not only stand against but they often make conquests of the *visible* church. It is only the *invisible* church of which Christ's description is true. Another instance is Eph. 1:22-23: "And hath put all things under his feet, and gave him to be the head over all things to the church, which is his body, the fulness of him that filleth all in all." Surely nothing false or evil could be part of the body of Christ, in whom God is well pleased. In spite of this double usage of the word "church," in and out of the Bible, we must remember that the true church, the saved church, the church in vital union with Christ, is the invisible church.

IV. *Other Qualities of the Church*

In addition to the description already given of the true, invisible church we find other characteristics mentioned in Scripture. The invisible church is:

1. Infallible (it knows its Master's voice and will not follow a stranger, John 10:5).

2. Indestructible (nothing shall separate it from

"the love of God, which is in Christ Jesus," Rom.
8:39; no one shall take it out of His hand, John
10:28).

3. Indivisible ("that they may be one, as we are,"
   John 17:11; "I am the vine, ye are the branches,"
   John 15:5).

4. Invincible ("the gates [defensive weapons] of hell
   shall not prevail [or stand] against it," Matt. 16:
   18; "the meek shall inherit the earth," Ps. 37:11).

5. Universal ("out of every kindred, and tongue,
   and people, and nation," Rev. 5:9; "the field is
   the world," Matt. 13:38; "God so loved the
   world," John 3:16).

Putting everything together, we would have some
such definition of the church of Jesus Christ as this:
It is the invisible, infallible, indestructible, indivisible, invincible, and universal body consisting of all
those who truly believe in and adhere to their Head,
the Lord Jesus Christ. In the vast majority of cases,
they are members of the visible church.

CHAPTER X

The Future: Gulf Between Two Worlds

I. Modern Views of the Future

Edwyn Bevan (*Christianity*, p. 224) says that some modern Roman Catholics, speaking off the record concerning their official doctrine of the endless punishment of the wicked, "teach that the punishment involves real pain, but that it is not forever, others that the punishment is really forever, but that it is not torment as pictured in the old view." This observation is even truer of the thinking and teaching of many Protestants. In other words, the tendency of modern times has been to take punishment out of eternity or eternity out of punishment.

Quite recently some seem to be trying to take the blessedness out of eternity also. If Hell is being changed into Heaven, Heaven is being brought down to Hell. Thus Paul Tillich ("The Meaning of Joy") finds joy and pain apparently inseparable. Moreover, for multitudes of thinkers Heaven must be presently, at least, a very miserable place, or state of mind; for God, say some, suffers because of the sins of His creatures. Being an infinite being, He must suffer infinitely and being omniscient He must suffer every moment. If He, who is the glory of Heaven, is infinitely miserable, it is difficult to believe that creatures, whose joy is in Him, could avoid being miserable also.

The traditional churches have not changed their creeds, but there can be little doubt that they have changed their preaching. Walter Lingle, I think it was, once wrote about "The No-Hell Church" where that doctrine had never been mentioned for more than twenty years. John Sutherland Bonnell said that it had been even longer in his Fifth Avenue Presbyterian Church. How many "No-Hell" churches exist, no one has dared to estimate. Hell is so dreadful that the very thought of it is well-nigh unbearable. At the same time, the conviction is growing that religion without a Hell is not worth much. It seems that the church can neither live with the doctrine nor do without it.

If the orthodox have been strangely silent about what they ostensibly believe, the neo-orthodox have decisively committed themselves to universal salvation. It is an irony of history that a movement which is often called Neo-Calvinism should repudiate the doctrine of particularistic election by which historic Calvinism has been distinguished. In a book recently translated into English (*Christ and Adam*) Karl Barth's implicit universalism is clear. Romans

5:1-11, he says, "only speaks of Jesus Christ and those who *believe* in him. If we read that first part of the chapter by itself, we might quite easily come to the conclusion that for Paul Christ's manhood is significant only for those who are united to him in faith. We would then have no right to draw any conclusion about the relationship between Christ and *man as such*, from what Paul says about the 'religious' relationship between Christ and Christians. We could not then expect to find in the manhood of Christ the key to the essential nature of man.

"But in vv. 12-20 Paul does not limit his context to Christ's relationship to believers but gives fundamentally the same account of his relationship to all men. The context is widened from church history to world history, from Christ's relationship to Christians to his relationship to all men" (pp. 87 f.).

It may be useful to contrast the universalism of Neo-orthodoxy with that of the older Liberalism. According to the latter, men do not deserve to be damned and therefore they do not really need to be saved. Or, if men do deserve to be damned, a loving God is morally incapable of damning them. So, after their measure of suffering in this world, with or without some further temporary suffering in the next world, all men are "saved." Neo-orthodoxy has too strong a note of orthodoxy to entertain such a view. It holds that man is sinful and does deserve the wrath of God. A reconciliation, however, can divert that wrath.

Such a reconciliation has been made in Christ, and it has saved or justified all men whom Adam's sin had damned. Faith is not necessary, according to Barth, to secure justification but only to experience the fruits of it. All men will sooner or later come to faith and thereby realize what they have always possessed but not previously enjoyed.

It has been characteristic of the sects to deny future punishment. Unitarianism emerged in this country basically as a protest against vindictive justice. It is true that this was not always in the foreground of the controversy, but it is probable that it was always in the background. In the debate over depravity and sacrifice and salvation, the great anxiety and offense was traceable not so much to these doctrines as to the fact that they led to vindictive and irremediable punishment. Universalism was explicitly and undoubtedly devoted to an attack on the particularism of New England doctrine. Most of the major present-day sects are opposed to future punishment. Some, like Jehovah's Witnesses, teach annihilation. The Mormons do not advocate annihilation, but most of their teaching either minimizes future punishment or says that only a handful of persons will undergo it. Christian Science, Theosophy, and other pantheistic groups know of no punishment that is not either ameliorative or illusory.

Although the traditional churches have tended to

be silent about endless punishment while Neo-orthodoxy has gone universalistic and the sects annihilationist, there appears to be a movement back to a reaffirmation of faith in this doctrine in our time. Carl F. H. Henry's statement that Jonathan Edwards' God is "angry still" is being recognized by many as true. Marcellus Kik finds the subject important enough to write a book on *Voices from Heaven and Hell,* as has Henry Buis in *Doctrine of Eternal Punishment.* Meanwhile Billy Graham and many others preach the doctrine around the world.

Perhaps Dr. Bonnell's *Heaven and Hell* is more symptomatic of our time and more indicative of the general trend. While repudiating what he feels are the excessive statements of Thomas Aquinas and Jonathan Edwards, there is a genuine appreciation by Bonnell of what he considers the neglected truth in this doctrine. While his book does not, in our judgment, do full justice to certain grim but undeniable realities, it is indicative of a far more candid evaluation of biblical eschatology than the naive optimism of a decadent Liberalism.

So much for the present lay of the theological ground. In this chapter we will restrict ourselves to a brief discussion of one point; namely, the fixity of the gulf between the two future worlds. There is an impassable gulf between these two worlds. If so, this is the death of any hopes of universal salvation.

II. Biblical Teaching About the Future

Our thoughts turn immediately to Christ's parable of Dives and Lazarus (Luke 16:19-31) in which this impassability of this gulf is stressed by Jesus. Describing Dives, the rich man, in Hell, and Lazarus, the poor beggar, in Heaven, Christ tells us that Dives is so miserable that he asks Lazarus (whom he sees in "Abraham's bosom," another word for Heaven) to wet the tip of his tongue. But this is impossible because, as Abraham explains in the words of the parable, "between us and you there is a great gulf fixed: so that they which would pass from hence to you cannot; neither can they pass to us, that would come from thence."

We recognize that we have here a parable. That is to say, this manifestly is not an exact description of the other worlds as they were at the time of telling the parable. For example, the parable has Dives in apparent physical misery, judging from the fact that he desires to have the tip of his tongue moistened. However, the Scripture indicates that bodies are not resurrected before the return of Christ. Rather, the bodies of the dead remain in the grave and nothing presumably happens to them except decay until they are later raised from the dead. Whatever the answer to that point may be we may be certain that there is this impassable gulf between the two future worlds. Jesus may be describing these future worlds by way of

anticipation; that is, He may be describing the condition of those who are in these worlds in a future
time when the final state of them has been established.
Or, He may simply be expressing in more easily understandable terms of bodily suffering the misery
which persons presently in Hell feel in their souls.
But we are citing this passage to show that the Bible
teaches the impassability of this separating gulf between the two future worlds. And this the parable very
clearly—and indeed emphatically—does, even though
it may leave us somewhat uncertain about some details. Regardless of whether this scene is taken to be
utterly metaphorical, whether it is taken to be an
anticipation of the future and final state of the two
worlds; or whether it is a description in bodily terms
of the present spiritual anguish of those in the evil
world to come, the one point with which we are concerned remains the same in all instances; namely, that
there is a wall of separation between these two worlds
and it is impossible to go from one world to the other
even temporarily.

Again, consider the passage in Revelation 22:11:
"He that is unjust, let him be unjust still: and he
which is filthy, let him be filthy still: and he that is
righteous, let him be righteous still: and he that is
holy, let him be holy still." Here the statement is
made that the filthy shall be filthy still. This tells us
plainly that there is to be no change in the evil
world which is to come. We know that in this present

world while there is life there is hope. So long as a man lives and the gospel is extended to him he may believe and be saved. Now is the day of salvation. But in very dismal contrast to that, the future world affords no such opportunity. There is no such possibility of a person entering into life which is everlasting. Just the opposite—if a man departs this world in sin, he shall remain in sin forever without hope of change.

Consider Hebrews 9:27: "It is appointed unto men once to die, but after this the judgment." We admit that this passage would allow a probation after this judgment. That is, the words themselves do not rule out such a possibility. However, they certainly do not assert such a thing and they do not imply such a thing. Furthermore, we find in Scripture elsewhere no support for the notion. So we are constrained to believe that the bluntness and the apparent solemnity and finality of this stark statement, "It is appointed unto men once to die, but after this the judgment," means to rule out later probation. That is the commonsense handling of this verse, and, in the absence of any information which would modify such a commonsense interpretation, it seems that we are shut up to such a construction.

Now if there is such a judgment which comes immediately at death and fixes the eternal abodes of those judged, then surely the two groups are eternally separated from each other, at least as far as intercom-

munication or interfellowship or transmigration is
concerned. One world may be conscious of another.
The heavenly world may be conscious of the hellish
world, and that consciousness may contribute to its
blessedness in some manner. Likewise the hellish
world may be conscious of the heavenly world and
that consciousness may contribute to its misery in
some manner. But, there is no going back and forth
from one world to the other, nor any fellowship between the two groups of inhabitants.

III. Source of Modern Errors

There is more Scripture to the same effect, but we
think this is sufficient to indicate the thought of the
Bible. Let us say a final word on this subject concerning the probable reason for persons' thinking that
there is a possibility of moving or progressing from
one world to the other, namely from the world of Hell
to the world of Heaven. As we are acquainted with
the history of doctrine, we suspect that it is not any
passage in Scripture which gives people such a notion;
rather it is the *feeling* that a future trial is necessary
at least for some people. That is, there are some
adults who have never heard of the gospel and therefore have never had the possibility of being converted.
Some theologians forget that these men who have not
heard the gospel had no right to expect that they
should hear a gospel; that there was no obligation on
God's part to present it to them. But, wrongly sup-

posing that all persons do have some right to a gospel and noticing that some persons have never actually been given that supposed right, these theologians are constrained to conclude that such a presentation of the gospel, since it has not taken place in this world, must take place in the other world. This opens up the possibility of persons in Hell believing and being saved and thus entering into felicity with the heavenly creatures and fellowship with God.

While we admit that this is, internally, a logically coherent pattern of thought, we say first that it is presumptuous to base a doctrinal affirmation, a dogma, upon something which is merely a very tenuous hypothesis. Second, and far more serious, however internally consistent this notion may be, it is destroyed by a false premise. We have reflected on the fact that some theologians assume that all men are entitled to a hearing of the gospel. This, however, is a gratuitous and erroneous assumption. God has no obligation to sinful men except to condemn. He may or may not, as His wisdom dictates, exercise mercy upon them. But mercy is not something which God must offer anybody. He offered no mercy to the angels when they sinned. And He says with respect to fallen human creatures: "I will have mercy on whom I will have mercy" (Rom. 9:18). He strongly insists that mercy is optional with Him and a matter of His sovereign pleasure alone. Therefore, it is extremely presumptuous for any man to assume that he has a right to

hear the gospel. Since we live in a land of light and
hear the gospel, we should be that much more grate-
ful that we have such an unmerited opportunity.
Furthermore, we should do what is in our power to
extend this opportunity to other persons. However,
neither we nor they may be said to have any right to
the good news. Neither we nor they, if we perish in
our sins, can justly blame God for not attempting to
rescue us from our sins. We are outlaws; we are
violators of God's will; we are spurners of the light of
nature and natural revelation which we do have. We
are entitled to nothing but Hell. If God leaves us to
that to which we are entitled, who will call Him unjust? So, however plausible-sounding this thesis of a
future probation may be, a careful examination shows
that it must be decisively rejected as erroneous and
presumptuous. And if this notion of a future probation is resting upon this erroneous and presumptuous foundation, then that which rests on it, namely
the possibility of passing from one world to another,
must collapse with its foundation.

But there is another side to this coin. If the finally
impenitent cannot ever pass into glory, on the other
hand, true believers cannot ever pass out of it. The
righteous shall be righteous still. So once again the
believers' eyes are on the Lord returning on clouds of
glory. "Even so, come, Lord Jesus!" For when He
finally takes His own to Himself they shall know that
sin shall never again separate them from Him; for

He has separated sin from them. ". . . between us and you there is a great gulf fixed: so that they which would pass from hence to you cannot; neither can they pass to us, that would come from thence." (See also Rev. 21:7.)

Now is the day of salvation. Let us, therefore, in conclusion consider what we must do now, since there is to be no opportunity to change worlds hereafter.

CHAPTER XI

The Way: Straight and Narrow

THE LESSONS ARE OVER. Now comes the homework. This is the "lab" part of the course. Here is where you learn by doing, having learned by reading.

Jesus tells us that, in spite of the glorious way of divine salvation, not many will find it. "Enter ye in at the strait gate: for wide is the gate, and broad is the way, that leadeth to destruction, and many there be which go in thereat: Because strait is the gate, and narrow is the way, which leadeth unto life, and few there be that find it" (Matt. 7:13-14). "Then said one unto him, Lord, are there few that be saved? And he said unto them, Strive to enter in at the strait gate: for many, I say unto you, will seek to enter in, and shall not be able" (Luke 13:23-24). "So the last shall be first, and the first last: for many be called, but few chosen" (Matt. 20:16).

Our Lord is not telling us these things in order to develop a curiously morbid interest in arithmetic. We are not to attempt a calculation of the number of the saved and of the lost. Rather, because we have been given advance information that relatively few will be saved, we are to see to it that we are among these. "Strive to enter in at the strait gate: for many, I say unto you, will seek to enter in, and shall not be able," says Jesus. Because there will be few who enter life, you are not to despair of entering, but to strive to enter.

Let us, therefore, address ourselves to this top priority matter of finding the straight and narrow path to life.

I. Recognize the Two Ways

Why has Christ told us that few will be saved? He did this to stress the urgency of being on the right road. As long as persons suppose that just about everybody is going to arrive, they will take the matter quite casually. They will not be concerned about it. They will tend to assume that they are on the right road, of course, and let things rest there. But when they are told that most people are on the wrong road and that relatively few are on the right road, it brings every one of us up short. It makes us ask immediately: How is it with me? Where am I going? Am I with the majority, calmly walking to perdition? How do I get on the right road? If there be few that find it, I had better start looking now.

The very first thing one must do is to recognize the simple fact that there are two different roads and that they lead to two different ends. As long as a person entertains the sentimental, popular notion that there are innumerable roads all going to the same place, there is no hope of his getting on the right road. He must recognize the fact that there are not many roads but only two: a right road and a wrong one. So far from going to the same destination, one leads to Hell and one to Heaven. This is a simple matter of fact. The one person who knows about these matters, Jesus Christ, has spoken on the subject. He came from Heaven and He has gone to Heaven, and He knows the way that leads where He is, and He knows the way that leads elsewhere. His word is clear, and His word is final. It is foolish to dispute it; the thing to do is accept it and act on it.

A young Hindu student studying in this country heard a speaker at an international group saying that Jesus Christ was the only Saviour of the world. Afterward he said; "I do not like your idea that there is only one way to Heaven—your Christian way. I like to think that there are many ways—your way and mine, the way of the Christians, and the way of the Hindus, and the way of the Muslims and of all religions. Your way is too narrow. I like room on the road I travel. I want other people with me, not just my own group." This all sounded very broad-minded. It was broad-minded. It was broad-road thinking. It leads to destruction. Not because the speaker said one thing and he said another; that is irrelevant. But Christ said one thing, and Hinduism says another. If Christ had said that men came to God through Hinduism, the young man could be right; but since Christ said, "No

man cometh to the Father but by me" (John 14:6),
the young man is dangerously wrong. He may want
a broad road with room for all faiths. There is such
a road indeed, but it does not lead where he wants to
go. He must simply recognize the fact that there are
but two roads, and they lead to different places. Until
he learns it, until you learn it, you are on the broad
road that leads to destruction. Jesus Christ ought to
know.

II. Get On the Straight and Narrow Road

You will never get on the right road until you
recognize that there are only two roads and that only
one of these is the right road. But recognizing this
fact is not getting on the right road. You have to find
it and enter it. You need make no effort whatever to
find the broad road. Men are born on that road.
They are born in sin and on the way to destruction.
Most of them stay on that road all their lives and
forever. Many of them never even think of getting
off while they still have an opportunity. They like
the road until at last, when it is too late, they see
where it leads. But to get on the right road real effort
is required. An act of the will is required once the
narrow road is found. No effort is required to remain
on the broad road. To make no effort is the best way
to stay on the broad road. It is the road of no
resistance; it is the course of the evil world that walks
according to the prince of the power of the air. But

the narrow road must be found and entered with
great difficulty.

Dante's *Inferno* tells of Virgil leading Dante to the
entrance to Inferno. There is a sign saying, "Abandon
all hope, all ye who enter here." There is a sign over
the entrance to the Kingdom of God also and it reads:
"Abandon all pride, all ye who enter here." All who
would enter this narrow road must abandon all pride.
They must recognize that they do not deserve to be
permitted to enter this way. They must know that
they have forfeited all right to escape the just damnation of their former evil ways. God is under no obligation whatever to rescue them from their Hellbound
way. He has every right to permit them to go on to
their destruction. The narrow road is a road of free
grace, of condescending mercy. No one ever deserves
to find or enter this way. Only God's grace can show
and open it. They must enter it in abject penitence,
with nothing in their hands, with only a plea of mercy
on their lips and in their hearts. "If any man," said
Christ, "will come after me, let him deny himself."
Let him pull himself up by the roots. Let him turn
away from himself and rely entirely on Christ. This
road is for sinners only. If a man has any righteousness of his own, an iota of merit or goodness to which
he can lay claim, the other road is for him. That is
where the supposedly virtuous make their self-righteous way to perdition. The road of life is for sinners

only—sinners whose hope is built on nothing less than Jesus' blood and righteousness.

A woman said to the preacher after listening to a sermon on this subject, "You make me feel so big," holding her thumb and index finger about a half inch apart. The minister replied, "Lady, that is too big." John Bunyan wrote in his autobiography that he found this road so narrow that there was room only for body and soul; not for body and soul and sin.

III. Agonize Along This Road

Not only must all who enter here abandon all pride but once they are on it they must agonize all the way to the end of it. It is a narrow road, exacting and confining. It is a road of holiness, and no sin is permitted here. It is for sinners only, to be sure, for those who know that they have no righteousness of their own and who trust in Christ alone. But they must, on this road, prove that they really do trust in Christ. And they prove this only by the striving after holiness. "If ye love," says the Lord of this road, "keep my commandments." Those commandments call for perfect holiness in every area of human behavior. Nor is there any time when a person takes a rest from holiness on this road. All the way he must be striving after his Christ who leads the way.

It is a road which calls for daily self-denial and bearing of one's cross. This is where the eye that

offends is plucked out and the arm that offends is cut
off. This is where the men of violence overcome every
barrier to their progress. This is where men hunger
and thirst after more and more progress along this
road. This is where men beat their bodies and keep
them in subjection. This is where the pilgrim presses
ever on and never counts himself to have attained.

Does someone ask: If there is the necessity of
"agonizing" and striving in the way, can it be a gracious way? Will we not be earning rather than receiving? Not at all! Suppose I were preaching in an audi-
torium and offered all hearers free watches on the condition that they would come down the center aisle to
get them. If they came down the side aisles, or
through the basement, or by a rear window, they
would not get the watches. Suppose they came down
the center aisle—the watches would be theirs *as a gift.*
They would not earn them by coming down an aisle!
They would only show that they would accept them
as a gift! So our persevering works only show our
entire trust in the free gift of God.

In spite of the rigor of this way so sharply in contrast to the ease on the broad road, this is a happy
road. Christ is this road and Christ is the companion
of this road. Those who bear His burden find that
the burden is light, and those who are under His yoke
find that His yoke is easy. Those who "lose" their
lives discover that they really "find" them. Those

who deny themselves, find themselves. Those who suffer are very happy. This, in spite of all its hardships and demands is the glory road.